life

without

stress

life

without

stress

The Far Eastern Antidote
to Tension and Anxiety

Dr. Arthur Sokoloff

BROADWAY BOOKS
NEW YORK

BROADWAY

A hardcover edition of this book was published in 1997 by Broadway Books.

Broadway Books titles may be purchased for business or promotional use or for special sales. For information, please write to: Special Markets Department, Bantam Doubleday Dell Publishing Group, Inc., 1540 Broadway, New York, NY 10036.

BROADWAY BOOKS and its logo, a letter B bisected on the diagonal, are trademarks of Broadway Books, a division of Bantam Doubleday Dell Publishing Group, Inc.

First trade paperback edition published 1998.

Designed by Julie Duquet

The Library of Congress has catalogued the hardcover edition as:
Sokoloff, Arthur.
  Life without stress : the Far Eastern antidote to tension and
anxiety / Arthur Sokoloff. — 1st ed.
     p.   cm.
  Originally published: Coral Gables, Fla. : Coral Publishers, © 1992.
  ISBN 0–553–06751–6
  1. Stress management.   2. Stress (Psychology)—Prevention.
3. Peace of mind—Religious aspects.   I. Title.
RA785.S686   1997
155.9/042—dc21   96–24920
                                                              CIP

ISBN 0-7679-0045-6

98 99 00 01 02 10 9 8 7 6 5 4 3 2 1

The true value of a human being can be found in the degree to which he has attained liberation from the self.

—ALBERT EINSTEIN

When the way comes to an end, then change. Having changed, you pass through.

—I CHING

C O N T E N T S

With true friends
Even water
Drunk together
Is sweet enough
—Old Chinese proverb

In bed be wife and husband,
In hall each other's
Honored guest.
—Confucius

This book is dedicated to my wife, Ruth, who initially inspired me to plan our first of many trips to the Far East. Subsequently, she was a cheerful and tireless companion during all our travels. As we visited shrines and temples far from the usual tourist's path, when we were stared at as seldom-seen Westerners, and when amenities were in short supply, her enthusiasm never wavered.

I'm grateful to her for her inborn sense of aesthetics, which increased my understanding of Far Eastern art, and for her contributions to the development of the lecture series, which are an integral part of this book. But most of all I thank Ruth for her encouragement and love, and her patience—which I am sure I stretched many times. In the most literal sense, this work never could have been done without her.

I also wish to express my gratitude to my parents, the late William and Belle Sokoloff, who early in my life instilled in me books and ideas. They encouraged scholarship and education, and saw to it that I received the very best of schooling that they could provide. My son, Dr. Terry Sokoloff, shares a portion of my thanks for countless hours of discussion about our mutual interests concerning the wisdoms of the West and the Far East, and how they interrelate. His assistance in some of my seminars and lectures was of great value.

AUTHOR'S NOTE

Western culture considers life to be a challenge, filled with problems to be solved and obstacles to be overcome. This viewpoint often leads to a feeling of unfulfillment, that something is missing from our lives. Taken to the extreme, this attitude can result in illness, ulcers, and heart attacks.

Conversely, the wisdom of the Far East teaches harmony with nature, rather than opposition to it. Obstacles and stumbling blocks are in fact stepping stones. Life *is* fulfilling, and we lack nothing.

This book offers insight into the wisdom of the East, presenting it in a readable, nonmystical, Westernized manner. It is meant to enrich, not replace, our traditional outlook.

From the moment we cease trying to swim upstream and begin to flow with the current, something changes within us. By combining our Western drive with the Far Eastern sense of tranquility and inner peace, we gain the best of both worlds. Our everyday lives are enriched, and we find that what we have been seeking was within us all the time.

Inner serenity is inner strength.

Introduction

A Window to the East

STRESS IS, LITERALLY, a killer. Until recently, the mechanisms of its workings were unclear, but we are now beginning to understand that prolonged frustration, anger, feelings of helplessness, grief, and other negative emotions cause the brain cells to produce chemicals that affect the entire body, including our immune system. With the body's defenses weakened, heart attacks, stomach ulcers, lower back pain, colitis, periodontal disease, and a host of other physical illnesses manifest themselves. The mind–body relationship becomes clearer when we recognize that stress influences the mind, which in turn chemically affects the other cells of the body.

Because I have practiced dentistry for enough years to have

treated four generations of patients, stress is not a stranger to me. Three of its many faces are especially evident.

Many dentists face, on a daily basis, psychological challenges that they are unable to cope with effectively. Depending on which statistics are used, my profession is at or near the top in the rates of suicide, divorce, alcoholism, and drug addiction. As the anxieties of my colleagues increase, their need to find solutions grows as well.

The dental patient enters the office with a certain—and expected—degree of apprehension. Known as white coat syndrome, this state of anxiety causes blood pressure elevation merely by being in a doctor's office. But those who blanch with fear, become angry, aggressive, or suspicious present a different problem. Their stress takes its toll upon their dentist, as well as upon themselves.

Most fascinating is the third aspect of stress as related to dentistry. Periodontal (gum) disease may actually be a barometer reflecting the anxiety level of the patient! Patients whom I have known for many years who suddenly undergo traumatic life situations such as divorce, loss of a loved one, or job loss may exhibit inflammatory gum conditions or even loosening of the teeth. Others, whose lives have been fairly tranquil, and who have a sense of well-being, will present a healthy periodontal condition. I have followed these records over decades, and the mind–body relationship—how excessive stress can

negatively influence our physical condition—is, in my opinion, beyond dispute.

The unfortunate truth is that stress and the problems that
cause it are here to stay. Global problems, such as pollution,
the environment, and the socioeconomic challenges that face
us on every newscast will not disappear tomorrow. The personal mental, emotional, and physical situations that belabor
our well-being will continue to come and go. Add to this a
background scene of day-to-day exposure to rudeness, noise,
traffic jams, and other annoyances and it seems a wonder we
survive at all.

Wonder is the right word. The toughness and adaptability of
the human mind and body is beyond comprehension. We
know that the effects of stress are dangerous, and we also
know that in most cases we cannot eliminate the sources of
stress. What we can do, however, is alter, diminish, and sometimes eliminate the effects imposed upon us by stress.

One way of looking at life is to see it as a continuing stream
of problems that need to be solved. Fortunately, Americans
are good problem-solvers. So, since the only way to avoid the
harmful effects of stress is to modify our response to it, how
do we begin? Do we acquire a sword to fight our opponent, as
in combat? Do we carry a shield to protect ourselves, as a defense? What can we do that hasn't been tried before in our
Western civilization?

This book is designed for those of Western background whose approach to life is pragmatic. Its purpose is to make available to us a vast realm of wisdom, as yet virtually untapped. The application of this knowledge has a direct, effective means of defusing stress and reducing its harmful effects. It is both a sword and a shield, and something more.

The Far East produced many sages and geniuses in its twenty-five-hundred-year history. This accumulated wisdom is largely untapped by our Western world because unfortunately, most of the writings and translations we receive are buried in mysticism and the esoteric. These qualities are turn-offs to most Americans. We prefer to face life's problems in a practical, logical, or reflective manner.

What happens to all religions is that as they evolve, the original concepts behind them become clouded. If the patriarch Abraham were to walk into a bar mitzvah at the Fontainbleu Hotel in Miami Beach, or Jesus were to walk into the Vatican, probably neither of them would recognize the beliefs they had brought to their people.

It is much worse in the Far Eastern religions. The line is very thin between the actual concepts taught by the Buddha, Lao-tzu, Confucius, and others and what has evolved since. Taoism is full of stories of people flying through the air, traveling (before subways) underground at great speeds, and living to be 200 years old or more. When these stories are

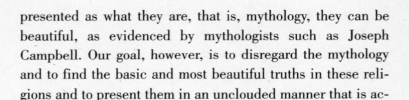

presented as what they are, that is, mythology, they can be beautiful, as evidenced by mythologists such as Joseph Campbell. Our goal, however, is to disregard the mythology and to find the basic and most beautiful truths in these religions and to present them in an unclouded manner that is acceptable to Western thought.

In writing this book, I have stripped away more than two thousand years of material that has clouded the original wisdom of the great thinkers of Asia. The Far East is mysterious only because we allow it to be so. What I've tried to do in these pages is provide basic concepts that Westerners can relate to and put to good use.

A Zen tale tells of a fish who was a Prince. One day he asked his mother, the queen fish, "What is this 'water' I keep hearing about? I don't know what it is!" The Queen Mother replied, "You were born in water, and you will die in it. It flows through you and around you. It is so much a part of you that you are unaware of it."

For those of us of American and European heritage, our Western civilization is very much the same as the water was to the fish. We are born into it and, with few exceptions, we go through life believing that our values, attitudes, and beliefs are somewhat universal. We forget that these cultural characteristics represent far less than half of the global population.

Awakening to the concept that all the world does not accept our values can come as a shock. Two incidents jarred me from my Western complacency and acted as catalysts to learn more about the rest of the world and how life is seen elsewhere.

Many years ago, I had occasion to visit a small village in another part of the world. Our guide–translator took us to a farm where I was introduced to the owner. He spoke to our guide, who translated to us, "Tell him that I have three white horses." As I looked over the area, I saw a poor tumbledown shack, poverty everywhere, and one horse. This horse was black, swaybacked, and showed through his thin ribs and worn hide every year of his hardworking life. "Why does he tell me that he has three white horses when he has only one, a black one, and miserable looking at that?" The reply from my guide, who knew well the culture of his country, and who was better educated than most, took a few moments to sink in before it stunned me. To this day, forty years later, recalling this incident brings back a shock of disbelief that filters through the decades. "In this civilization," my translator replied, looking into my eyes as if to see the effect his answer would bring, "In this civilization the truth is not important."

I had been raised on classical Greek philosophy, and for many years Socrates, Plato, and Aristotle had been my imaginary mentors. Years of college-level Western philosophy augmented my earlier love of the subject. And if any one theme carries through from the earliest pre-Socratic thought to modern analytic philosophy as the highest value, it is the love and pursuit of the truth. And here was an entire culture, perhaps one-sixth of the world's population, in which the truth was not important! I had never before stopped to think that my beloved, truth-seeking Western philosophy was far from universal. The wisdom of the West is in fact only one form of wisdom, and I had come face to face with that fact.

On another occasion I was doing business in China and learned how bewildering and confusing a different civilization may be if one is not familiar with their cultural heritage. I overheard a conversation between two businessmen, an American and a Chinese, and the dialogue went something like this:

American: That is a beautiful watch you have!

Chinese (smiling and nodding): Thank you.

American: I would like to buy it from you.

Chinese (still smiling and nodding): Yes.

American: I would guess it is worth $500.

Chinese: Yes.

American: I'll meet you here at seven o'clock this evening and pay you
  for it.

Chinese: Yes.

The conversation then proceeded to other, unrelated subjects such as family, and my attention wandered. It refocused, however, when the conversation drew to a close, for it was then that I heard:

Chinese (still smiling): This watch is not for sale; furthermore, it is worth $1,000!

As you may imagine, a business agreement conducted in such a manner would mystify anyone engaged in commercial dealings who did not understand one basic fact: With the exception of some merchants, such as those in Hong Kong, who are used to dealing with Westerners, in most situations, when a Chinese smiles, nods his head, and says "yes," he is not saying "Yes, I agree with you." He is saying, "Yes, I hear you," or "Yes, I hear what you say." This is not being evasive, nor tricky, nor in any way dishonest. He is simply following a centuries-old tradition of nonconfrontation that is rooted in the religion and philosophy of his culture. Anyone without knowledge of these traditions is at great disadvantage in a business enterprise.

Such dialogue within a business transaction reveals an even deeper level of culture than what appears on the surface. The entire process is a stress-free expression of compromise. There is no confrontation, no loss of face, no forced backing down by either side. There is respect for the other's ego, cordiality on both sides, and mutual agreement at the conclusion. I know of high-level Japanese-American trade negotiations where, at the point of a confrontational crisis, the Japanese call for tea and a break in the discussions. Frustrating for the Americans, but a normal, tension-breaking procedure for the Japanese.

Such customs are anchored in the religions and philosophies of the Far East. They permeate and color virtually all aspects of life, bringing with them the sense of serenity much needed in the West.

The tensions of our daily lives are increasing, and our ability to cope with them often appears inadequate. The mental and physical damage caused by stress is well documented. Are our traditional Western religions and philosophies adequate to shield us from everyday pressures?

For some of us, the answer is yes. We have access to psychiatry and psychology, along with their offshoots, such as group counseling and related therapies. For many people religion is a major source of relief from anxiety; we all know someone who possesses such deep religious faith that their inner strength prevails over the deepest tragedy. Newer methods include health clubs at which one can work off the tensions of the day, aroma therapy, music therapy, and other relaxing treatments. And of course there is a vast assortment of drugs, both legal and illegal, which offer temporary relief.

Those who find these Western means sufficient to assuage the pressures of our modern environment are indeed fortunate. But there are many for whom feelings of disillusionment, inadequacy, frustration, uneasiness, and isolation are daily companions. For this group, the wisdom of the East may provide a storehouse from which people can glean the inner tranquility necessary to face today's society. Twenty-five hundred years of accumulated wisdom concerning an approach to life, continually refined and perfected by some of the world's greatest philosophers, is a formidable ally in our daily life. It is within reach of most of us.

From Taoism, we learn about our own inner nature, and how such an understanding provides a deep sense of harmony and tranquility within us.

From Buddhism, we learn the causes of human unhappiness and the treatment that logically follows.

From Zen Buddhism, we enhance our intuitive abilities and are able to cut through seemingly endless complications to the very heart of a problem.

And from Confucianism, a sense of who we are and where we belong develops, which leads again to the inner tranquility we all seem to seek.

In learning the concepts and practices of Eastern philosophies we are opening the gates to a vast treasure of wisdom, born and cultivated in the Far East and just beginning to be known and understood in the West.

All good Oriental art reflects the underlying beliefs and attitudes of Far Eastern thought. Huston Smith, who has taught world religions for more than fifty years, told Bill Moyers on a recent television program that in the Eastern hemisphere "the art is the religion, and the religion is the art."

What better way to utilize art than to relieve stress? The visual imagery available to us is not only free, but we may recall it in our mind's eye whenever it is needed. "And then my heart with pleasure fills, and dances with the daffodils," wrote Wordsworth in his poem "Daffodils," recalling a pleasant scene in the English lake district. We can follow a similar path.

The absolute serenity reflected in Buddha's face can evoke the same response within ourselves. A sense of our oneness with nature arises when we picture the Taoist yin–yang symbol, the dark and the light intertwined in an eternal bond. A recalled vision of a lotus flower floating, pure and untouched, on muddy waters helps us to imagine ourselves rising above unpleasant situations or surroundings.

Imagery is of prime importance in the Far East, since in earlier years most of the population could not read. The art was designed to go straight to the heart of the observer, evoking spiritual and meaningful feelings. It can do the same for us, so I will call upon it from time to time.

There is an adage that states "Bored people are boring people." The corollary to this is that "Interested people are interesting people." It is challenging to see the world from a perspective different than that with which we grew up, and challenges of this sort stimulate us and in turn make us more stimulating. To be able to see a play, movie, or news event concerning the Far East and to comment on it with a degree of genuine understanding makes us better conversationalists and intellectual companions. The ancient Romans said that the purpose of education is to keep from being bored, and to avoid boring others.

It is one thing to read and to study cultural attitudes that are different from our own. It is another thing, however, to learn about the wellsprings from which these attitudes arose, and how to view the world through Eastern eyes.

If only the smallest part of our minds can begin to think as a Far Easterner would, if we could shift our outlook from Occidental to Oriental when we wish, then a whole new world would open up. We will have at our command not only the wisdom of the culture we were born into, but the wisdom of an entire other hemisphere as well!

Before we begin our journey, I would like to offer this word of assurance. When most of us think of the religions of the Far East, we picture a gleaming, jewel-bedecked Buddha in a remote Asian jungle. Rudyard Kipling and Indiana Jones have given us these beautiful and exotic images, and I have traveled many miles to explore these esoteric wonders. But the fact is that the basic concepts of these religions, once stripped of the superstition, legends, and myths that have built up in layers over the centuries, require only common sense and a little work to understand.

Great truths are essentially simple. When we suddenly gain an insight into what had seemed a complex scientific or philosophical problem, we say to ourselves, "But this is so basic! I should have known it all along!" Once we begin to understand the universal truths inherent in Eastern philosophies, we will be able to tap into our own inner strength and begin to find our way to inner serenity.

1

Empty the Cup!

Do not worry about tomorrow,
for tomorrow will worry about itself.
—MATTHEW 6:34

THERE IS A Zen story that tells of a professor who lived in a university town in Japan. He was an authority on all subjects, from mathematics to history. The one thing he did not know about was Zen. Determined to include Zen among all his other scholastic achievements, he visited a Zen master who lived in a small cottage on the outskirts of the town. The master, venerable Nan-in, invited him in and, as was the custom, served tea. He filled the professor's cup until it was full, but then kept pouring until the tea overflowed the cup, ran over the table, and began to spill onto the floor. The professor watched this until he could no longer restrain himself. "The cup is full! No more will go in!" "Exactly!" replied Nan-in. "Your mind is like this cup. It is so full of your ideas and opinions that there is no room for me to show you Zen!"

Our minds are very much like the professor's. Born into the cultural heritage of the West, the greatest hurdle we must overcome is to allow new ideas, strangely different from our own, to enter and be accepted into the framework of our thoughts. Close your eyes and imagine a full teacup inside your head. Then, if you can remove even one or two drops of the tea, you will have room to gain even a little insight into some Far Eastern beliefs.

What are these beliefs, and why are they so difficult for us to grasp? The following concepts are the four that seem to present the greatest obstacles.

Four Strange Ideas

These ideas are strange only to us. To almost half the world, they are as natural as breathing.

Multiple Religions

Most people in the Eastern hemisphere believe in two, three, or even four religions, all at the same time. They feel no conflict at all with this. This is the equivalent of asking someone in our Western society:

"Are you a Roman Catholic?"
"Yes. I attend Mass regularly."
"Are you a Baptist as well?"
"Of course!"
"And are you a Jew?"
"I certainly am!"

To us, this is a ridiculous conversation. But the fact is that most Chinese are Taoists, Buddhists, and Confucianists, simultaneously. Most Japanese are Shintoists and Buddhists, living in a highly Confucianist society, with some Japanese being Christian as well, giving them four religions. But most startling of all is that they see no conflict! I have spent many hours discussing this with people in the Far East and the reply is invariably so simple and direct that I cannot fault it: "If one religion is good, then two are better, and three are better yet!" This is an idea totally alien to us. They usually go on to say that they cannot understand why Westerners each practice only one of the many religions available.

Our Asian friend will also remind us of our bloody history of religious wars: Catholic against Protestant, Christian against Muslim, and wars between sects of the same religion. Religious warfare is almost unknown in the Orient. They simply do not understand our behavior regarding religion, and acting as an informal spokesman for the West in these conversations, I can offer only the weakest of explanations when trying to account for violence in the name of religion.

Acceptance of Opposing Concepts

We are raised and taught to think in straight, logical lines. If something is one thing and that thing only, it cannot be something else. Philosophically expressed, it would read:

"A is only A."
"A is not B."

This is perfectly rational to us, and we accept it without much further thought.

In the Eastern mind, however, this bit of elementary Greek logic does not necessarily hold. They may say:

"A is only A, and not B."
"A is B."

This pair of expressions is absolutely incomprehensible to any Western logician. How can two ideas, opposite in nature, be true at the same time? Yet in the Far East, this is seldom a point of dissension. We will come to realize this more in future chapters as we learn, for example, that two of the basic

Chinese religions, equally recognized and observed, are exact opposites in intent and practice. These are Taoism and Confucianism, both forming the substructure of Chinese culture.

Contributing to this dilemma is the language itself. The nature of the Chinese language is obscure, relying on suggestion and imagery for many of its expressions. For example, "total darkness" may be written as "under the raven's wing." Language will be discussed further in later chapters, but we can begin here to grasp the relationship between the language and the thought. The artistic, creative, and imaginative attributes of Oriental writing are immeasurably enhanced by the nature of the language itself. But precise, definitive, logical patterns of thought are more easily expressed in English, French, and other European tongues.

Religions without Gods

Christian, Jew, or Muslim, we are inclined to center our religion on a supreme being or god. Our interpretation of this god changes as we grow older. As children, we are apt to perceive God as a father, perhaps with a long white beard. As we grow, this image is apt to change to a more generic idea of a creator. Depending on the religion itself, our upbringing, and our own thoughts, our idea of who or what God is changes several times for many of us as the years pass. He is frequently seen as the giver of moral and ethical laws such as the Ten Commandments, which must be obeyed. Success or failure in following these laws can result in reward or punishment accordingly. Even those who do not follow traditional religious beliefs as they mature may have vague feelings of guilt should they break a commandment. These feelings can often be traced back to early childhood, when the dicta "Thou shall . . ." and "Thou shall not . . ." were firmly implanted.

It is rather startling for most of us, then, to find that in some of the major religions of the Far East there is no god. In historical Buddhism, for example, the Buddha is not a god. The Buddha was a man and frequently referred to himself as such. Religion without a god seems a self-contradictory concept, but as we explore the Oriental framework of beliefs, we will gradually come to understand how this may be.

Religion and Philosophy Are One

It is traditional for Occidentals to keep their religion and philosophy separate. Each of us may have our own religion and an unrelated philosophy as well, should we so choose. One may be a Roman Catholic and a pragmatist. Someone else may be a Methodist and a neo-Platonist, or a Jew and a logical positivist. Generally speaking, unless one is ultraorthodox in their religious commitment, the religious and philosophical aspects of their lives do not encroach upon each other.

In the Eastern hemisphere, however, another set of concepts exists. The religion and the philosophy are one and the same. A Taoist claims the Tao as both aspects of his life simultaneously. A Confucianist lives his religion as his philosophy, as does the Buddhist and the Shintoist. There is no differentiation. So we see that not only do most Far Easterners have multiple religions, but that each religion has a philosophy as well.

As we progress and gain insight into Eastern culture, these four strange ideas will become increasingly more understandable and, in turn, we shall become more comfortable with them. It is even possible that we may begin to see some value to them, a value that we may translate into an enrichment of our everyday lives. Albert Einstein said that common sense is nothing more than deep-seated ideas we acquired before the age of eighteen. He was referring to scientific research, but perhaps it applies to the study of foreign culture as well.

Before we know where we are going, we must know where we came from. This knowledge provides us with a basis of comparison as we examine the culture of the Far East.

Culturally, where do we come from? It would take an army of historians, scholars, and psychologists to attempt to answer this question, and the answer would still be incomplete. The fabric of our Western society is so complex that no one can describe it. The threads of this fabric reach endlessly back through time and space to ancient civilizations, through the arts and politics and wars of peoples in distant lands thousands of years ago. And each thread of this fabric has strands that stretch back into prerecorded antiquity.

Fortunately, we can identify the main bulwarks of our Western culture. The origins of how we think and what we value can for the most part be described in terms that are not distantly alien to us.

We Are All Greek

A bold statement, perhaps, but true. Anyone born, raised, and educated in Europe, America, or other parts of the world where Western civilization predominates, derives most of their culture from the ancient Greeks. Our democracies, architecture, fine arts, patterns of logical thought, justice and morality, and our outlook on life in general is Greek. Any American walking down Constitution Avenue in Washington, D.C., is looking at Greek columns on most of the federal buildings. And in the smallest of towns or county seats, chances are that the town hall will have similar Doric, Ionian, or Corinthian supports. In addition, many portraits of George Washington and other great Americans feature poses based on the Greco–Roman ideal of a gentleman farmer called to the defense of his country.

How did this happen? The rise of Greek civilization in the

seventh, sixth, and fifth centuries B.C. transformed the world. Art, architecture, writing, government, commerce and trade flourished. But it was during the fourth century B.C. that Greek philosophy reached its highest development. The philosophy created by these Athenian masters embraces us to this day. Socrates, born in 470 B.C., was the teacher of Plato. Plato, in turn, was the teacher of Aristotle, who was the tutor to Alexander the Great. And Alexander conquered almost all the known world, thereby spreading the Hellenistic culture and its values.

But before we consider briefly just what this philosophy is, let us turn to a lesser-known Greek philosopher who lived before Socrates, Thales of Miletus, who is regarded as one of the seven wise men of ancient Greece. Thales lived in Miletus, the olive-growing capital of ancient Greece. Evidently, he was subjected to ridicule for being more concerned with abstract ideas than with the real world, so he decided to do something that would end the scoffing. Using his knowledge of science and weather, he predicted an early harvest for the olive crop. He then proceeded to lease all the olive presses available and, when the olive harvest arrived, he held the monopoly on their pressing. In one season he became a rich man, thereby proving to his detractors that philosophy had practical applications.

I confess to feeling a special kinship with Thales since, for many years, I, too, have been chided by friends and acquaintances for being involved in philosophy. Many people believe that philosophers live an ivory-tower sort of existence removed from the real world. Some people think I should be out golfing or discussing the stock market rather than bumbling around with dusty old books. But like Thales, I know that philosophy has practical applications.

In this book, we will be studying the religions—which are also the philosophies—of the Eastern world, and what we learn will be useful in our everyday lives.

There are 168 hours in a week. Most of our waking hours involve work, homemaking, sports, and other daily activities that may create a tremendous amount of stress. I suggest that the hours spent reading this book should be spent as though you were a philosopher. Relax, get comfortable, and read with an open mind; as new ideas begin to flow, you will instantly begin to feel "de-stressed." Like Thales, we know that philosophy, far from being useless abstractions, has practical application to our daily concerns. Furthermore, as Socrates taught in his outdoor lectures, philosophy (which literally translates as, "love of wisdom") is for *all* people, not just for a few professors in universities.

One of Plato's famous parables tells about a cave in which a group of men are chained together in a row facing the wall. They cannot turn around, or see in any other direction. Behind them is a fire which casts the shadows of these men upon the wall. To them, these shadows are the only reality. One of the men, however, breaks free of his bonds and runs to the entrance of the cave. There, under the blazing sun, he sees the real world. If he were to reenter the cave and relate his discovery to the remaining prisoners, his description of the outside world would make no sense to them and they would, in fact, consider him to be either witless or insane.

So it is in our daily lives. We all go about tending to our chores and duties, and enjoying our pleasures and recreations. Most of us, most of the time, accept the things we see and do at face value, much like the prisoners accepted the shadows in the cave as reality. But if we occasionally take a little time to contemplate or to question what we see or do, then we are like the man who escaped—we begin to see things as they really are, illuminated by the sunshine of knowledge and truth. We are, under those circumstances, beginning to think like philosophers.

What the Greek philosophers sought to attain, we still seek today . . . the Good Life. To this end, they pursued three main ideals: Truth, Goodness, and Beauty, which they believed would bring them to their goal. In seeking the truth, they studied logic. In seeking goodness, which may be interpreted as morality, justice, and proper conduct, they studied ethics. In seeking beauty, they studied aesthetics.

Since this is not a book on Western philosophy, we will elaborate further on just one of these concepts. Logic contains many tools of thought that are used to guide us on a straight path towards the truth. One of the simplest, yet purest instruments of logic is known as the syllogism. We will discuss it only briefly here, because in a later chapter on Buddhism we will encounter a religion that is based on a thought process so lucidly syllogistic in nature that it could be attributed to the Greeks.

The Greek syllogism, perfected by Aristotle, usually consists of two statements known to be true, from which we can then deduce the truth of a third statement. The classic example is:

Man is a rational animal. (major premise)

Socrates is a man. (minor premise)

Therefore, Socrates is a rational animal. (conclusion)

Or we may say:

Alligators like to eat meat. (major premise)

Albert is my pet alligator. (minor premise)

Therefore, Albert likes to eat meat. (conclusion)

The clarity and purity of logical thought leaves no room for superstition or mysticism. That is why Buddhism is sometimes called the "thinking man's religion," since it is based primarily on what seems to be a series of logical statements.

It is also interesting to note that parts of the Talmud, which is the sacred book of Judaism, were written by Hellenized Jews, that is, Jewish scholars who had studied Greek logic after Alexander the Great had conquered that part of the world. They used applied logic to explain and interpret the Five Books of Moses in the Bible.

Our Judeo-Christian Heritage

This brings us to the second element of our Western culture— our spiritual and religious backgrounds. We cannot deny the major impact that our Judeo-Christian heritage has on our civilization to this day. We know that an Old Testament saying is inscribed on our Liberty Bell in Philadelphia. In many cases, even nonobservant Jews or Christians will feel guilty upon breaking a commandment. And how many of us raise our eyes heavenward when a wish is granted or a disaster averted? It is simply built into us as a part of our spiritual and cultural heritage.

Pragmatism—The American Philosophy

The third component that contributes to our Western cultural patterns applies primarily to Americans. It is a philosophy known as pragmatism.

The United States has given several cultural gifts to the world. Probably the most well known is jazz. Born in New Orleans, developed and enriched in Memphis and Chicago, this distinctive sound has been widely exported. Our second major cultural contribution is some of our modern art. In the 1950s, for the first time in history, more American art was exported to Europe than European art was imported into the U.S. Jackson Pollock, de Kooning, Alexander Calder, and many others have influenced the art world in both hemispheres.

And as novice philosophers, readers of this book should take pride in our philosophical export, pragmatism, as well. Just what is this American-grown philosophy? Since this is not a book about Western philosophy, we will deal with it as briefly as possible, capturing its basic concepts superficially, but with enough meaning to grasp how it influences all of us.

The best way to do this is by relating a story told to me as a student many years ago at Case Western Reserve University; it illustrates the essence of pragmatism so well that it remains with me to this day. Daniel Boone, the great American pioneer and explorer, is the hero of this tale.

It seems that he awoke hungry one morning and taking his rifle in hand, set out into the forest in search of game for breakfast. Soon he spotted a squirrel on the trunk of a large oak tree, and he pointed his rifle toward the squirrel. At this, the squirrel ran swiftly to the opposite side of the tree trunk, out of sight of the hunter. Boone immediately moved behind the tree, but the squirrel countered by running again to the opposite side. This continued in such a manner that if Boone moved either right or left, the clever squirrel immediately raced to the opposite side of the trunk, thereby remaining out of sight and no longer presenting a target. This continued for a while, much to Daniel Boone's annoyance.

But what has this to do with philosophy? The *philosophical* question asked here is this: If Boone continues to circle the tree, facing it, moving to both the right and the left and, if the squirrel continues to counter-move in such a way as to always be on the opposite side of the trunk out of the hunter's sight, then is Daniel Boone going around the squirrel or not?

This question can be argued in two ways. On one hand, we may say that since the squirrel is on the tree and remains there, and Boone is circling the tree, then he is going around the squirrel. On the other hand, since the squirrel cleverly remains on the opposite side of the trunk, moving continually out of sight, then Boone is *not* going around the squirrel, only around the tree. Such is the *philosophical* argument, which could continue endlessly.

Along comes pragmatism, like a breath of fresh air, which says: "The wrong question is being asked, and a stupid one at that! The question should be: 'Does he get the squirrel or not?' " In other words, pragmatism places its value on the efficiency and successful application of an idea: Does it work?

Founded in 1905 by Charles Sanders Peirce and William James, pragmatism was often ridiculed by European scholars who called it the "American businessman's philosophy." But the fact is that Americans are a practical and can-do sort of people. We have produced inventors such as Thomas Edison, Henry Ford, and the Wright Brothers. Anyone recalling World War II remembers feats such as the Navy Seabees arriving on a remote jungle island and in twenty-four hours completing a landing strip for Air Force use. We may complain about our telephone service but, as any experienced traveler will tell you, we have the best in the world. We have landed men on the moon and probed the depths of the seas. Perhaps the most common, everyday experience that illustrates America's technological skills is the feeling of pleasure when our car starts in the morning at the first turn of the key.

There is a story about an English country gentleman who one day became absolutely elated when he discovered that all his life he had been speaking prose! Similarly, most of us are pragmatists, but don't know it until it is pointed out to us. The basic concept of pragmatism, which takes philosophy out of the abstract and theoretical realms and tests it by practical application, is an integral part of most of us.

Some years ago I was fortunate to be able to spend a few days with a world-recognized American philosopher. I held him in special esteem because he had a grasp of both Eastern and Western beliefs. I had always wondered what his personal choice was, but he had never answered this question during his hundreds of worldwide lectures. One evening, however, at a party at which he had had enough wine to "loosen his tongue," I asked him, of all the philosophies, which was the one he found most satisfying? "Of all the philosophies I know," he replied, "my personal choice and the one I live with is pragmatism."

From the Greeks, we have inherited the concept of the Good Life. We value truth, justice, and beauty. Our love for freedom and democracy is rooted in our cultural Greek ancestry.

From our Judeo-Christian heritage comes our religious and spiritual background, reflected in our art, morality, and basic cultural concepts.

Pragmatic values influence us daily. "Let's try it this way and see if it works" is as American a concept as any we might conceive.

Obviously, this is far from being a complete account of our Western cultural heritage. But these three Western influences will be used as reference points as we examine Far Eastern philosophical concepts in the chapters which follow.

The Major Difference

If I were asked to reduce this entire book to its simplest terms, it would be this: The difference between the Western mind and Eastern mind is that Westerners see themselves as superior to nature, opposing it and dominating it. Eastern man, on the other hand, sees himself as a part of nature, identifying with it and being at one with nature.

How on earth did we ever get the idea that we should oppose or conquer nature? This is another one of those questions that cannot be readily answered. But we can come up with one very valid possibility: our own Bible. In Genesis 1:28 we read, "God said 'Fill the earth and subdue it. Have dominion over the fish of the sea and the birds of the air and over every living thing that creepeth upon the Earth.' "

If we subdue and have dominion over the earth, then we are setting ourselves apart from nature. This apartness, this sense of being separate from the rest of the universe, often leads to a feeling of loneliness or desolation. True, the benefits of putting ourselves above nature result in many scientific advances for which we are rightly and truly grateful, but this is a double-edged sword. The further we drift from nature, the more we are isolated from our roots, the more we are condemned to a sense of uneasiness about where we really belong.

The great anthropologist–poet–essayist Loren Eisely often bemoaned our sense of isolation from the very nature from which we have sprung. I had the good fortune to know Loren Eisely, and I regret to this day not telling him something about the Far Eastern view of man and the universe. It might have eased his mind to know that the other half of our planet sees things quite differently.

All the religions, philosophies, art, beliefs, and attitudes of the Eastern hemisphere revolve around the concept that we are a part of, a creation of, and should strive to be in harmony with nature. As we shall see, this feeling leads to a sense of inner peace and tranquility that can transcend our daily lives.

It is with these thoughts in mind that we enter the world of Tao, which best expresses these ideas, and in fact forms the underlying theme for much of the wisdom of the East.

2

Going with the Flow

At peace with Heaven and Earth, and at One with the Tao.
— *L A O - T Z U*

THE ABILITY TO transport ourselves through time and space in our mind's eye is usually taken for granted. Let us use this unique gift to begin our journey to the Orient by first turning back the clock to the sixth century B.C. Now let us place ourselves in China. We are in a large, dense forest. It is midwinter, and snowing heavily. Looking more closely, we see a man seated under one of the snow-laden trees, carefully observing the scene. This man's name is Lao-tzu, and what he is thinking now will change the thinking of almost half the world.

Let us pause for a moment, and consider the nature of genius. One of its qualities is the ability to observe something seen by countless others, but to draw from it a viewpoint hitherto unknown. Sir Alexander Fleming in the 1940s saw mold growing on bread, a common sight to all, and from this continued on to the discovery of penicillin. Sir Isaac Newton, as the humorous legend goes, was sitting under an apple tree; when an apple fell on his head, he "discovered" gravity. As Sherlock Holmes remarked to Dr. Watson, "We see, but we do not observe."

These are, of course, oversimplified summations of important incidents. What actually occurs is that scientists dwell, both consciously and subconsciously, on these problems for long periods of time. At a given moment, precipitated by a minor incident such as Newton's falling apple, everything falls into place in a flash of insight, and a giant step is taken.

And so it was with Lao-tzu, a wandering teacher and philosopher. What did he see, and how did it awaken in him a new understanding? How much of this tale is myth or legend and how much is truth are arguable points, but the scene described and how the venerable master reacted to it has philosophical, if not historical, merit.

As Lao-tzu (literally, "Old Master") observed the falling snow collecting on the many branches in the forest, he became aware of two things. The sturdy, strong branches held

the snow without giving or bending, until eventually the accumulated weight caused these branches to snap and break.
The younger, more supple branches, on the other hand, gradually bent with the weight until the snow slid off onto the
ground, and the branches returned, unharmed, to their original positions to repeat the process.

What does this have to do with the philosophy–religion
known as Tao? Tao, which literally means "way," is used to
represent the entire cosmos or universe. From the smallest
blade of grass at your feet to the most distant galaxy a million
light years away, all is Tao. It is constantly moving, changing,
and creating. It is beyond description and understanding; it
cannot be explained. "The Tao that is spoken of is not the
Tao."

What did Lao-tzu see in his snow-laden forest to relate to
Tao? He realized that since we are part of the Tao, it is futile
to try to go against it, just as the unyielding branches tried to
"oppose" the snow. Those branches that were supple, bent
with the weight of the snow and survived. But since the Tao is
so vast and unknowable, what are we to do?

The wise person studies the Tao, which in modern writing
is sometimes equated with nature. By doing so he comes upon
certain aspects of nature that are knowable. He then tries to
lead his life in a manner that is in harmony with nature, rather
than opposing it. Attempting to go contrary to the Tao is akin

to scratching your nails on a chalkboard. Young people today have an expression that describes this perfectly: Go with the flow.

Since this was an agricultural society at the time, it is easy to see how farmers observed the seasons of nature following each other in a natural order. Plants sprouted in the spring, grew in the summer, needed harvesting in the autumn, and the earth rested in the winter. Any farmer planting at the wrong time was doomed to failure. He was going against nature, or the Tao.

At this point we come face to face with our Western minds. We are out to conquer nature, but the Taoist sees the wisdom of living in harmony with it. The real strength is to give in, to bend with nature. Frequently, water is used as the ideal. "Water is stronger than granite; you can cut granite, but you can't cut water." Paintings also illustrate water's strength. They paint such scenes as a storm-tossed warship, filled with hostile, armed, aggressive warriors, sinking below the waves, as the yielding, giving water quietly covers all.

Another frequent comparison used to illustrate Tao thought compares a newborn child to a very old person. The newborn is flexible and supple, which is the nature of life, whereas the aged becomes increasingly stiff and immobile as death approaches. The quality of bending or yielding reflects the nature of life, or perhaps the life of nature, or perhaps the life of nature as seen from the Taoist view.

Most of the Far Eastern martial arts, such as karate or judo, have roots that reach back to the Tao. Western combative sports feature two boxers or wrestlers coming head-on to each other in the ring, two forces opposing each other. The basis of most of the Far Eastern martial arts is to step aside as the opposer attacks, and to use the attacker's own energy against him, perhaps adding a push or tripping maneuver to accelerate his fall. The students of these activities are trained mentally as well as physically. Such concepts as centering and being at one with the enemy contribute to the mastery of the martial arts.

The "bible" of Taoism is a book attributed to Lao-tzu known as *Tao Te Ching*, usually translated as meaning "The Way and Its Power." It consists of about eighty-one short poetic writings. Some are concerned with politics and government, some with our own personal lives, both within ourselves and in our relationships with others, but all are as relevant today as they were twenty-five hundred years ago.

Now we have some grasp of the fundamental vision of the Taoist, who sees the universe as one vast, constantly changing entity in which all things are truly related. He also believes the wisest way to live is "to be at one with Tao and at harmony with Heaven and Earth;" a Taoist holds that the aim is not to conquer Nature, but to live in harmony with it.

Our next step is to seek out those values of Taoism that we can adapt in order to improve our everyday lives. This is to be

achieved by avoiding mysticism and superstition, and trans-
lating the original wisdom into a pragmatic and useful form,
ready to be assimilated into our modern Western culture.

The best way to achieve this, in my opinion, is to select
three of the most universal and practical subconcepts of Taoism from the volumes of Taoist literature. The three ideas that
follow, readily relate to us today.

Your Inner Nature

If we are a part of the entire universe, or nature, or the Tao,
then it stands to reason that a small portion of this Tao lies
within each of us. It is, in fact, our own, personal bit of the
Tao. It is individual, unique, and one of a kind. No other being has the same part of the universal Tao as you do. This is
called, in Taoist literature, the "te."

Te is a good term to use, but we can translate it into a more
commonplace term: your own personal, inner nature. The
rather nebulous idea of living in accordance with the Tao becomes much easier to follow when we realize that all we have
to do is to live in peace with our own inner nature, or te, which
is really a part of the Tao. Your inner nature contains your own
true character, your virtues and powers, unaffected by social
pressures and outside conditions. But because from birth on-
wards, society forces us into so many molds, we can lose sight

of our true nature. Behaving outside our nature seldom leads to happiness.

An experience in my own life illustrates this point. Many of my friends are good golfers, and for more than two years it seemed proper for me to play with them. But the truth is that I have no ability in or real interest in golfing; I was miserable and frustrated on the days I did play with them, but I went along to be sociable. One day, however, I realized that I was going against my own inner nature, and it was causing me much unhappiness. I found that spending those half-days doing things that I enjoyed, such as preparing lectures or reading, freed me from the anxieties of golfing and enriched my life in other ways. I was in harmony with my te!

We are all different. Some of us are sociable and enjoy parties and gatherings of all sorts. Others are happier being alone, reading or watching television. Some are physically active; others are not. Some are scientifically inclined, others artistically so. It is not a matter of one trait being better than another; it merely is an acknowledgment of what we are. Our true inner nature is our best guide.

Obviously, our work should reflect, if possible, our natures. We know that an introvert will not make a good salesperson and that an extrovert will be frustrated hidden behind a desk or on an assembly line. But this presents us with another problem. What do we do if upon examining our inner selves we find characteristics that we don't like or that may not be good for us? Once again, my personal experience may be used to illustrate an answer.

I am not only a poor golfer, but an all-around nonathlete as well. Sports and physical activities have no appeal for me; yet I am reminded daily that exercise is important for good health, and couch potatoes are doomed to early extinction. What is to be done if my te is in conflict with what I know to be best for me?

The first answer is what *not* to do. Do not make a strenuous effort to override your basic nature. To make a vigorous resolution to become an athlete starting tomorrow will not work, and may be harmful. Yet one cannot simply sit back, do nothing, and blame it all on one's inner nature. This is one of the flaws and dangers of believing in astrology. A friend of mine is a Virgo. When he is told that he is nitpicking, he is apt to reply: "That's what Virgos do! There is nothing I can do about it!"

If, upon examining our inner nature, we find something we don't like, we should plan a change, but one that is gradual and kind to ourselves. Refusing to change is nothing more than a cop-out. I may not play tennis, but if I walk, or bicycle, or do some yoga exercises daily, I can get my exercise in a pleasant way, and perhaps even begin to like it. This is much more effective than a radical approach and, to use a pragmatic expression, it works. The message of the te to us is to live naturally, being true to your own nature. If you do wish to change something, do it gradually and with a sense of kindness to yourself. There is a bit of the Tao in Shakespeare, as Polonius counsels his son Laertes: "To thine own self be true, / And it must follow, as the night the day, / Thou canst not then be false to any man" (I, iii, 78–80).

Keep It Simple

Another Taoist teaching that holds potential benefit for modern Americans is the idea of "p'u," which translates as "the uncarved block." If go with the flow relates to the Tao, and inner nature is our te, then keep it simple is the modern expression for p'u.

An old Chinese tale tells of an artist of such skill and ability that his fame became widespread. One day he painted a picture of a snake that was so perfect and lifelike that a viewer might expect it to jump out of the picture. The passion of the artist was so intense that he could not stop; he painted feet on the snake. This expression, "painting feet on the snake," has become a Chinese adage. It refers to situations that are made more complicated than they need to be. We can be happier people if we reduce the complexity of both our outer and inner lives.

We all know that mechanical appliances, from radios to telephones to automobiles, become more and more complicated each year. Gadgetry is added continually to make us dissatisfied with what we have, to desire the new model, and to make us wonder how we ever got along without that extra row of buttons whose function is not quite clear. We also know that this increases the price of the product, but what is worse is that as things become more complicated, there are more parts to break down, and greater cost of upkeep. Instead of laborsaving devices giving us more time to enjoy our lives, we are usually seduced into working longer and harder to pay for them, and spending more time and money having them repaired.

But our personal selves are more important than mechanical gadgets. When our inner selves become more and more complex, when we drift further and further from our basic nature, which is, in fact, simple and childlike, there is a penalty to pay. For it is the child—nature that has the most fun, that looks out upon the world with wonder and awe, that enjoys life. How many times have you seen a child discard a complicated toy and play for hours with the box it came in?

Simple does not mean foolish. It means returning to the basic values of life which are plain and self-evident. It means acting spontaneously and intuitively. Sometimes our wonderfully logical Western mentality can lead us astray, giving us false values. At times we should try thinking with our hearts rather than our heads.

Sometimes, when caught in a traffic jam, I look at the people in the cars around me. Frequently, in a new, expensive, status-inspired automobile, a young person will be talking nervously on the car phone, with the radio blaring stock reports and business news. The look on his or her face is one of tension and anxiety, frustration and unhappiness. It seems that these adult toys do not always bring much peace to the owner. An automobile can be a wonderful place to relax. If we are stuck in a traffic jam, we can sit back in the comfortable seat, turn on pleasant music, adjust the air conditioning or heat, and turn the time into a few minutes of contentment and quiet, not often found during a workday. Depending upon material possessions for our happiness becomes a sort of "painting feet on the snake" for our inner selves. After a while, these things own you; you don't own them.

Doing By Not Doing

This brings us directly to a third major area of Taoist thought, known as wu-wei. This is interpreted as meaning nonaction, or doing by not doing. A bit of this philosophy injected into modern American attitudes would be a blessing.

There is a sort of self-induced frenzy in most of us that persuades us, once we have awakened, dressed and eaten, to pursue a sort of frantic busyness. We work, we jog, we rush to social events, and pursue a host of other activities as if the world depended on us. Sometimes we try to do more than one thing at a time, like talking on the phone while driving the car, or listening to educational tapes while running, or having a business or "power" meeting during lunch. (Whatever happened to the idea that lunchtime can be spent pleasantly conversing with a friend, or quietly reflecting alone, away from the concerns of our daily work?)

This concept of needing to keep busy is nonproductive, greatly reduces our ability to enjoy and appreciate life, and is outright dangerous. The cartoon character Ziggy recently observed that the formula to achieve success is the same as the formula for having a heart attack. But the words that most wisely illustrate the point at hand come from Matthew 6:28–29: "Consider the lilies of the field, how they grow; they toil not, neither do they spin. Even Solomon in all his glory was not arrayed as one of these." We don't have to be busy all the time; just being ourselves is of worth. The lilies don't have to prove their worth by work; they add to the beauty of the world just by being themselves.

There is nothing wrong with hard work, or wanting to succeed, or having ambition. I frequently think of the sign over the Mayo brothers' desk in their original office at the Mayo Clinic; it reads: "There is no fun like work." I agree wholeheartedly.

The concept that morning-to-night busyness is what gives

us our worth is wrong, and so is the loss of perspective that follows from this concept. The doctrine of wu-wei tells us that things can sometimes get done without us, that we don't have to be everywhere and on top of everything at all times. Things evolve and change continually, and sometimes doing nothing gets the best results. Bernard Baruch achieved part of his fortune by doing nothing on Rosh Hashonah and Yom Kippur. Once, on one of those days, his advisors vigorously urged him to alter his market holdings, but he preferred to observe the holiday in the traditional manner by not working. The market did the exact opposite that his advisors had predicted, and his fortune skyrocketed by doing nothing.

And so wu-wei gives us the message of following the Tao, or nature, in all our activities. Work is fine, but should be taken in the context of our entire lifestyle, not as a totally consuming drive towards some far-off goal. To be ourselves, to allow time for pleasure, relaxation and simple enjoyment of our families and the world about us leads to the Good Life of the Greek ideal. A physician who has attended the deathbeds of many people once remarked, "I have never heard a dying person say he regretted not having worked more or harder during his life."

The Art of Tao

All good Oriental art reflects the beliefs and attitudes of the people. Taoist art incorporates beautifully what we have learned, and becoming familiar with it brings a double benefit. First, by understanding what we are looking at, we increase immeasurably the pleasure derived from the viewing. Seeing Eastern art through Western eyes deprives us of much of the gratification we should expect. Secondly, the painting itself transmits its message, and if we are even a little receptive, the painting will "speak" to us.

The typical Tao scene shows a landscape, usually with peaked mountains fading into the mist. There will be trees and rivers, and often cliffs and valleys as well. But looking more closely we will see, tucked into the hills, a small village, and human figures, frequently a sage and his students, blending in with the overall landscape.

One of the achievements of Western art was the development of geometrical perspective; that is, making objects appear to be more distant by making them smaller. Eastern art, especially that of Taoist influence, prefers what is called atmospheric perspective, creating a haze or mist which gives the illusion that mountains, streams, and other objects are partially lost in the distance. This lends to the overall message of the painting: that man and his creations, such as the village, are a part of the natural surrounding, not prominently displayed in front of it. We seldom see a *Blue Boy* or a *Mona Lisa*, with the human figure dominating the canvas as the landscape fills in the rest. A Taoist painting portrays nature, with man in his proper relation to it, a part of nature blending in with the whole. Once a few of these have been viewed, they become easily recognizable.

Recently, in the National Art Museum in Beijing, China, my wife and I visited a display of modern art designed to represent the current socialistic standards. To our great surprise, the exhibit included a large painting so Taoist in flavor that it could have been done a thousand years ago in the Tang or Sung dynasties! I couldn't believe this had been allowed, until my wife pointed out to me something I had overlooked. Winding down the side of one of the peaked mountains was a tiny army motorcade with tanks, trucks, troop-carriers, and ambulances. Clearly, the artist had created a perfect Taoist painting and, to make it acceptable to the Communist regime, had incorporated a modern military scene!

Also frequently incorporated into the art are the symbols of the yin and the yang. The flag of Korea, as anyone who watched the 1988 Olympic Games televised from that country will recall, has as its center the yin–yang design. This consists of a circle divided in half by an S-shaped line; one half of the circle is light colored, the other dark. This symbol, without which no study of the Tao would be complete, is the artistic representation of a major aspect of Taoist thought.

The yin and yang represent the two opposing principles of the universe; both of which are needed to complete the celestial "soul." Male and Female, Heaven and Earth, Sun and Moon, Light and Darkness, Vigor and Passivity, Odd and Even . . . these dualities, in which the first is the yang element, and the second the yin, constitute the basic Taoist view of the cosmos. The Tao is the universe, which cannot be described, but the yin–yang principle derives from it and is used to describe the phenomena with which we are familiar.

This theme pervades Chinese art, and much of its science and medicine as well. Mountains are yang, while valleys and streams are yin. The traditional dragon is yang, but the dragon with the divided tail is yin. If you see a Chinese plate decorated with peaches, it possesses yin quality, as suggested by the cleft in the peach. Foods also contain yin and yang qualities, and a balanced diet will have proper amounts of each.

This sense of harmony, balance, and proportion permeates Taoist behavior and is reflected in everyday life for the Taoist.

Incorporating Taoist Thought

Now that we have a workable understanding of the Tao, the time has come to face the primary purpose of this book, and to adopt and use some of this wisdom in our own lives. This is our American pragmatic nature at work. Can the Tao be of value to us in our modern, fast-paced society?

There is no doubt that absorbing even a small amount of this Eastern wisdom can, for many people, bring about an inner tranquility that offsets the ever increasing stresses and pressures of our times. This becomes a matter of seeing the world in a slightly different way, one that alters our perceptions of events and of ourselves. It is easy to say, "Let's change our attitude," but exactly how do we do it?

Like anything worth having, this change in viewpoint requires work. The work is not difficult; however, it requires some persistence. To an open-minded person, this challenge is fascinating. Can I, born and raised in Western culture, allow even a little Far Eastern wisdom to enter my thinking? We are not going to replace any of our Western philosophy; we seek to add to it, and enhance it. Anyone who can face a business problem, interpersonal situation, or deeply personal crisis while acknowledging and allowing for two different points of view has a decided advantage.

The Tao shows us how to rework our perception of ourselves in relation to the universe, or to nature. This simple step, once achieved, can bring about a sense of relief from anxiety, from loneliness in the world, from a sense of isolation. We are not removed from nature; we are truly a part of everything, from the farthest galaxy to the flower growing outside your window.

But we have no magic switch in us that allows us to say, "From now on, I will see myself as a part of nature, not as one removed from it, or superior to it, or charged with dominating, altering and subduing it." So where do we begin? Home is the best place.

Anyone who has a pet usually sees himself as lord and master of the animal and its welfare. But suppose we try to regard our dog, or cat, or other pet in a different light. If we are religious in nature, we may say "we are both creations of God." Others may begin to regard the animal as a companion rather than a possession. True, the pet may be dependent upon us for its food and shelter, but that does not mean that we own him. We are, in fact, different aspects or manifestations of nature. We share the same need of sustenance to live. We are both born, and we both will die. The fact that one depends upon the other does not make one superior to the other.

The plant kingdom offers us equal opportunity to change, in a subtle and gradual way (although some people do this rather quickly), our perception of ourselves relative to the universe. My own personal experience came in the Muir Woods north of San Francisco. This occurred years before I became aware of Far Eastern thought, and I really didn't know what was happening. As I stood there in the swirling and fading mist, dwarfed by the giant redwoods with their trunks and limbs reaching heavenward, I suddenly became at one with my surroundings. As we shall see in the following chapters, this awareness may envelop us gradually or suddenly. The results are the same either way; only the means is different.

But we don't need giant redwoods as our plants to achieve this. A small garden or flowers in a window box will do. Perhaps there is a cluster of trees nearby, or a planting arrangement that pleases us each time we see it. As with our pets, as we care for our plants, or stroll by a particular tree, we should feel a kinship, rather than a distant and superior relationship.

Different people will find that different methods work for them. You may feel this oneness with nature while gazing at a flower, or watching a sunrise, or being nuzzled by a kitten. But whatever the means, even the faintest sense one acquires of being in harmony with the universe should be gently cultivated and allowed to grow.

Using the Tao to Disarm Stress

Having acquired a general knowledge of Taoism and three of its central concepts, te, p'u, and wu-wei, and having spent a few minutes daily trying to relate to nature in a manner different from the usual Western approach, we are now ready to face a major problem of our society. I refer, of course, to stress.

First, we must review the dangers of stress. Both mental and physical breakdowns, heart attacks, ulcers, high blood pressure, and a host of other ailments are frequently stress-related.

Second, we must face the fact that the chances are slim that stress-inducing situations will be controlled in the near future. Crime, drugs, the environment, traffic jams . . . all these contribute to the tensions of our daily lives. This is worsened by personal problems, relationships, business and financial matters, health problems, and a host of other factors which combine to push us nearer the breaking point. There is only one condition over which we have control: our own mental makeup and how we handle the stress. We may not be able to change the anxiety-producing elements; an unpleasant supervisor or an overbearing relative are difficult to dismiss easily. But how we cope with the pressure is what counts, and it is in this area that the Tao becomes our ally and asset.

We cannot minimize the Western methodologies which have developed over the years. Psychiatry, psychology, and related techniques such as group therapy, prove effective for many of us. The comfort of religion is enormous for some; just recently I read an article in the daily paper about the role of religion and faith in the life of Loretta Young, whose tranquil beauty is evident at 76 years of age. No one can discount the role of religious faith.

Drugs, both legal (such as alcohol) and illegal (such as marijuana) can be stress-reducing, though often at a bitter price. A recent trend, both wholesome and effective, is the health spa, where thousands of adults work off their acquired tensions via exercise and aerobics. Some of us blow off steam by watching a ball game, while others may turn on quiet music and kick off their shoes. We have developed an array of stress-reducing techniques that work for many.

But for others, these approaches are not enough, as the increasing incidence of stress-related conditions indicates. There is no reason why the wisdom of the East cannot be utilized and adapted to our needs; Western technology and ideas have certainly altered life in the other half of the world.

Before we apply our new knowledge to the problem, we need some understanding of just why stress is mentally and physically harmful. Since this is not a book about physiology, a superficial but basically accurate description will suffice.

Once again, let us turn back the clock, this time to one hundred thousand years ago. Our common ancestor, early man, emerges from his cave and finds himself face to face with a saber-toothed tiger! At this point, a miracle brought about by millions of years of evolution takes place in an instant. Faced with life-threatening disaster, hormones pour into the bloodstream, blood pressure increases, muscles tense, heart rate speeds up, the shoulders hunch forward slightly, and a host of other biochemical and physiological changes occur. The body's entire metabolism has changed in seconds to prepare him for one of two options: fight or flight. If armed with a club, and if he makes the quick judgment that he can kill the tiger, he will fight. If unarmed and defenseless, he will opt for the second choice, and turn and run as fast as he can. Either way, he will burn up the store of instant energy nature has provided him with, and he will survive. This stress response is a survival mechanism, for which we must all be grateful. We have all read of incidents where a mother, whose child is trapped beneath a car, lifts the automobile enough for the child to escape, a feat that would be impossible for her to do under ordinary circumstances. This classic example of the fight-or-flight response shows us that nature prepares us wonderfully for either choice.

Now let us move our hero forward in time to the present, exchange his fur loincloth for a blue suit and oxford button-down shirt, and place him in a modern threatening circumstance. His boss has called him into his office and, albeit unfairly, accused him of not doing his work satisfactorily, hinting at his dismissal.

The clothing may have changed, but not the genetic, physiological response mechanism of his ancestor. Once again, the adrenaline flows, and the same reactions take place. But it is at this exact point that the danger occurs. The cloak of civilization has masked his options; he can neither fight nor flee. He may wish to pick up an ashtray and hurl it at the boss's head. Perhaps he would rather turn on his heel and leave the room, muttering the familiar "take your job and . . ." as his parting statement. Neither option will work; he cannot resort to violence, nor can he just quit since he has responsibilities to himself and others. Meanwhile, his mind and body are pumped up by his stress reaction; with no release, it will begin to take its toll. We can go through this many times with no harm done, but compounded with other daily frustrations, from traffic jams to an argument with a loved one, day after day, our mental, physical, and general biological makeup begin to suffer. High-tech, transistorized, modern civilization has its price, and it is a steep one.

What can one do? The best answer I ever read to this question was by a cardiologist from Michigan, who was quoted in a popular news magazine. "If you can't fight, and you can't flee, then flow." He reinforced that idea by also stating: "Don't sweat the small stuff. And it's all small stuff."

Does the word "flow" ring a bell? It is the essence of Taoism; to be at one with the Tao is to flow with it. This is indeed a marriage of ancient Chinese philosophy and current Western treatment for our self-destructive tensions and anxieties.

Let us now give ourselves a "final exam" by hypothesizing a potentially stressful situation, and then drawing on our knowledge of the Tao to determine how to confront it in such a way that the potential damage to our physiological and psychological selves is minimized.

There are two kinds of people in the world, nourishing and toxic. Being with the former is like a plant being watered. We feel a sense of well-being; their positive, fulfilling manner, optimistic nature and pleasant company are uplifting. We welcome them, knowing instinctively how beneficial it is to be in their presence.

Toxic means poisonous, and that is exactly what toxic people are. Their cynicism, sarcasm, and demeaning and aggressive natures literally poison our psyches, making us feel depressed, anxious, unworthy, and generally down. We all know such individuals, and it is best simply to avoid associating with them.

However, life is not that easy. We are frequently bound to such unpleasant relationships. Whether it's with an office manager or coworker, a member of the family, or someone else we are forced to come in contact with frequently, the results can be devastating. We cannot change the situation or the toxin bearer; however, we can change ourselves. More specifically, we can change how we perceive the confrontation, and how we will handle it. This is where thinking like a Taoist comes in. We are not becoming Taoists; we are merely using a Taoistic attitude for a short period of time to defuse a potentially damaging situation.

As for the situation itself, we might imagine ourselves as a mechanic, who has done a good repair job; however, a few days later the customer returns and angrily and unfairly criticizes the work. Or perhaps we are a salesperson who is about to face an antagonistic, fault-finding shopper, and our anxiety is already beginning to build.

But for this situation, let us select a truly toxic person personified by an aunt, who is going to spend a few days with us. In this case we cannot "fight" by simply refusing to let her stay with us; such refusal would jeopardize domestic tranquility. On the other hand, we cannot "flee" by moving into a motel and leaving her alone in the house; this would be interpreted as an insult. To protect ourselves from damaging stress, we need to learn how to "flow."

We must envision the attitude emanating from this person. Whatever form it takes—sarcasm, aggressiveness, criticism, ridicule, etc.—we must prepare mentally to meet it. But to let it hit us outright is dangerous, nor can we duck or run away from it. We must "flow," or to be more precise, let it flow through us. This is where the Taoist's frequent reference to water becomes useful. If we can create a mental picture of momentarily becoming water, this barrage would simply pass through us. Water also takes the shape of whatever vessel it is in; it can adapt to any situation. Its true strength lies in its ability to go with the flow, to let difficulties pass through harmlessly.

This is where the incident of the smiling Chinese businessman described in the introduction becomes important. If we nod our head and say "yes" during the onslaught, only you will know that you are saying, "I hear you," and not "I agree with you!" What effect does this have on the opposition? It deflates and frustrates their aggressiveness, since they were expecting to collide head-on with you. Imagine a boxer coming into the ring, expecting to meet his opponent face to face. Instead, he finds himself in a ring filled only with fog. He swings wildly, but makes no contact with anything. His force is dissipating, and there is little he can do. Whatever mental imagery works for you, be it fog, turning into water, or merely going through the motion of nodding and saying yes, this learned behavior can be cultivated and improved. It is, in fact, momentarily adapting a Far Eastern approach to problem solving, as opposed to our Western solution of squaring off for a head-on collision. What is most important, however, is that it serves to deflect the causes of the stress, which is to our own benefit. And to sum it up in our own pragmatic view, it works!

The aftermath of such behavior is apt to be a situation wherein the person causing the stressful incident blows off steam. In the case of the mechanic or salesperson, a more reasonable conversation can follow, leading to some sort of agreement. When one is compelled to associate with a toxic person, we can adopt this attitude of flowing whenever necessary.

The values to be learned from the Tao may be summarized thusly: Whenever we must choose an option, make a decision, or pick a direction, we should take into consideration our te, or inner nature. We should think of p'u, which is the simplest answer. The more complicated a solution is, the more there is to go wrong. And wu-wei, doing by doing nothing, is always a possibility. There are times when it is the wisest move.

But it is in the underlying concept of the Tao, that we are a part of nature, or the universe, that its strength lies. From the very first moment that we begin to see ourselves at one with our surroundings, the sense of isolation and distance begins to crumble, our anxieties lessen, and it becomes easier to go with the flow. The aim is not to conquer nature, but to live in harmony with it.

The Tao was born in China twenty-five hundred years ago. It is still one of the three major religions of the country. At first, the Communist regime banned religious activities strenuously, but more recently has loosened its grip to allow many Taoist temples to function. Although this philosophy–religion has remained within China's borders, its basic concepts are to be found in most Far Eastern thought. Buddhism and, in particular Zen Buddhism, have their roots intertwined with the Tao at many levels. In fact, the Tao is sometimes referred to as the "mother" of Zen.

We will now introduce ourselves to Buddhism, a philosophy that enriches most of the Eastern hemisphere.

3

A Serenity That Surpasses All Understanding

Strive with diligence, and be a lamp unto yourselves.
—*BUDDHA*

I KEEP A copy of Omar Khayyam's *Rubaiyat* next to my bed, and I frequently enjoy reading a few verses before falling asleep. One of my favorites is XXVII:

> *Myself when young did eagerly frequent*
> *Doctor and Saint, and heard great Argument*
> *About it and about: but evermore*
> *Came out by the same Door as in I went.*

Nowhere in my readings is this theme better expressed. We may attend lectures, seminars, and classes in philosophy, but when we again enter our daily lives, nothing we have studied alters, improves, or refreshes our normal existence. Sadly, this applies primarily to most Western philosophy of today; it is essentially sterile.

I don't think this is the way it was meant to be. When, as a boy, I was first attracted to these studies through such classics as Will Durant's *History of Philosophy*, it seemed to me that the ancient Greeks felt philosophy to be of public interest and benefit. In my youthful fantasies I saw myself with Socrates, clad in white robes, asking passers-by on the street such questions as "What is Justice?" or walking through Athens with Diogenes and his lantern in broad daylight, searching for an honest man. Western philosophy began as public debate and dialogue, and from it grew such wonderful ideas as democracy and social justice—concepts that truly have re-shaped history.

By contrast, modern Western philosophy is mostly an ivory-tower mentality. While I have great respect for the mathematical, logical language that has been developed and for those who have pioneered these endeavors, only a very few people can exchange thoughts and ideas so conceived. These studies are distant and unrelated to our everyday lives, so we tend, as Khayyam said, to enter and exit through the same door.

Far Eastern philosophies are living philosophies in that they relate directly to our daily lives. They permeate our thoughts, activities, and decisions in such a way as to improve both our personal and interpersonal lives. That is why it is worth learning about them. Modern Western analytic philosophy has its place and value, but when it comes to basic human problems, few answers are to be found therein.

Buddhism is one of these living philosophies. As we face again a Far Eastern view of life and its problems, we should review our basic approach. Buddhism, like Taoism in the previous chapter, will be presented divested of almost all the layers of mysticism, superstition, and mythology that accumulated through the centuries. This is accomplished by drawing the material from the oldest records known, those closest to the lifespan of the Buddha. This is not to be perceived as an effort to demean mythology, which contributes much to the richness of all our cultures and civilizations. Any reader of Joseph Campbell's works knows the wealth of mythological insights.

We separate fact as much as possible from myth in order to reveal the inherent wisdom of the basic philosophy to the late twentieth century reader. Some mythology is retained when it enhances the narrative and enriches a particular scene described, but it will be clearly identified. The factual story itself does not require embellishment.

Buddhism is sometimes referred to as "the light of Asia."

From its inception in India twenty-five hundred years ago, it spread to China, Korea, Japan, Tibet, Thailand, Cambodia, Vietnam, Sri Lanka, Laos, Indonesia, and other Far Eastern countries. It was carried by merchants and priests traveling over the ancient trade routes.

It is also called the "thinking person's religion," since it is based on concepts of reason. The Buddha was not a god; he was a man, and frequently referred to himself as such. He often referred to his purpose as being similar to that of a doctor. In Buddhism, there is also no savior, nor are there miraculous or supernatural events; there is no heaven or hell, nor divine commandments to be obeyed. The Buddha was a human who discovered what was, for many of his followers, a path to reduce the unhappiness of the human condition. Possessing no supernatural or divine powers, he was seen by himself and others as a guide along that path, someone who points the way.

The Life of the Buddha

The historical Buddha was, in fact, born a prince in a small kingdom in northern India about 500 B.C. His given name was Siddhartha. His two other names are Gautama, which refers to his clan, and Sakyamuni, which refers to his tribe. Sakyamuni means the "sage of the Sakya tribe." These names are worth remembering, since they often appear in literature and art as alternatives to the term Buddha. In his early life, he is called by any of these names, or referred to as the prince, since he did not become the Buddha until later.

His mother, Maya, died a few days after giving birth. It is the manner in which his father, King Suddhodana, decided to raise his son that provides some insight into his future. The prince was to be brought up under conditions which virtually isolated him from the miseries of the outside world. He was never to be allowed to see old age, poverty, illness, or death. A wall was built around the palaces to ensure that his father's orders would be enforced.

The prince grew to young manhood under these conditions. He was handsome and tall, with bronze skin and attractive features. Athletically adept, he excelled in the sports which were popular at that time, including archery, javelin and discus throwing, and horsemanship, among others.

Mentally, he was equally adept and well trained. The best tutors, provided by the king, taught him the philosophies, languages, literature, and classics of the time. These he absorbed rapidly, becoming conversant with almost every subject known.

He married Yasodhara, a princess from a neighboring kingdom, who bore him a son. And so he lived, until he was twenty-nine years old. It was a life of sensual pleasure and indulgence, totally sheltered from the real world. Female minstrels followed him, and lived in the several palaces his father had built. He knew nothing but luxury and gratification of the senses, but something was about to happen that changed all that.

One evening, Siddhartha asked his charioteer, Channa, to take him outside the walls. Having been given orders by King Suddhodana against this, Channa refused. But the prince's will prevailed, and soon they drove through the gates. Crouched outside was a beggar, ravaged by disease and showing the sores and lesions of his illnesses. Not having seen anything like this before, Siddhartha asked for an explanation. Channa replied, "This is a condition that happens to many of us sooner or later." Disturbed by the sight, the prince returned to his palace.

On the following night they left again. This time they encountered an old woman, bent over, walking with difficulty, and supporting herself with a stick. Again the prince asked for an explanation, and Channa answered, "This is old age, a stage that comes to all living beings."

On the third night a funeral was in progress, and as they passed the procession of mourners, they viewed the corpse. Asked what the meaning of this was, Channa again replied: "This comes to all men."

The prince was filled with sorrow, and was fully aware that until this point his life had been one of wasteful self-indulgence and indolence. He determined not only to change his life, but to find the cause of human suffering and the means to end it. But how was he to do it?

He had seen something else while outside the palace, mendicants or ascetics. In many religions throughout history, there have been sects that believed that mortification of the body would benefit the soul, that to acquire spiritual wisdom, one must ignore and demean the physical self.

These ascetics wandered singly or in small groups, seeking salvation. The prince decided to join in such an endeavor.

The Great Renunciation

In Buddhist art, there are some scenes possessing such dramatic and emotional impact that they were repeated often in many media, ranging from a bas relief on an ancient temple wall to a silk-screened painting. *"The Great Renunciation"* is such a scene. It depicts the prince as a man who has reluctantly chosen to leave his beloved wife and son in order to pursue a spiritual mission.

He has decided to do this while they are asleep. Two reasons are given for this; he could not bear to see their sadness upon his departure, and he did not completely trust his own determination, thinking it possible for them to dissuade him. With utmost tenderness he bids farewell to their sleeping forms, and leaves the palace.

At the edge of the forest, where he had come with Channa and his stallion, Kanthaka, the prince removes his jewelry and robes, exchanging them for a beggar's rags. He cuts his hair, bids farewell to Channa, and disappears into the forest.

The Mendicant

He joined a small group of ascetics, and began a life of self-denial and a search for spiritual insight. They sought out sages with whom they studied; they lived by begging, always on the edge of starvation.

For six years the wandering continued. Self-deprivation had taken its toll, for Siddhartha was nearing death. It is said that his hair was long and matted, that dirt fell off his body in cakes, and that one could see his spine through his stomach. His diet had been reduced to one drop of water and one sesame seed a day. But in spite of all the physical denial and the continual studies, nothing had been gained.

Siddhartha, realizing that nothing further was to be gained, left the group, which derided him for doing so. He arrived at a river where he bathed, and washed and cut his hair. Nearby, a girl, Sugata, was tending cows. She brought him a bowl of rice and milk, which he devoured, his first normal food in six years. This scene not only illustrates a turning point, but sets the stage for the first basic concept of Buddhism.

The Middle Way

Siddhartha now established a pillar for the religion he was later to introduce. He was aware that just as it is useless to lead a life of total indulgence, luxury, and sensual gratification, it is also nonproductive to go to the other extreme of self-denial and physical deprivation. To achieve any sort of goal, especially spiritual insight, we need a clear mind and a healthy body, in other words, the middle path or way. This theme underlies the whole of Buddhist thought, as we shall see later.

This concept appears in our Western teachings as well: "Moderation in all things." Even the Boy Scout motto, "A sound mind in a healthy body," reflects this feeling.

Siddhartha was now thirty-five years old. He had still not achieved his goal. But his determination had become even stronger, and his spiritual drive to find the key to solving the problem of human unhappiness had peaked. His next step would change half the world.

The Enlightenment

Proceeding to Bodhgaya, and selecting a large tree, he sat beneath it in a cross-legged position of meditation. The tree is known as the Bo tree, which in fact is a member of the ficus, or fig tree family. The particular species is called *ficus religiosa*. In Bodhgaya, India, trees which are claimed to be descendants of the original bo tree are pointed out to travelers.

This is the high spiritual peak of the Buddhist religion, the religious equivalent to what Moses receiving the Ten Commandments on Mt. Sinai is for Judaism, or the crucifixion of Jesus and His resurrection are to Christianity. Siddhartha Gautama Sakyamuni, in a pose that is familiar to all of us when we visualize the Buddha, had resolved to solve the problem of human suffering and unhappiness.

Mara, the god of the underworld, did not wish to see the prince succeed. At first he sent his armies up from the depths to frighten the prince, but as they approached, they and their weapons of war turned to flower petals and floated to the ground. His second attack released hordes of devils, goblins, and other netherworld beings to force Siddhartha to abandon his quest. But they, too, turned into fragrant, drifting blossoms.

It was then that Mara played his ace. He sent his three daughters, Desire, Discontent, and Passion, to dance before the prince seductively, but it was to no avail. Realizing he was powerless to prevent what was about to happen, Mara retreated. The Buddha-to-be pointed his hand downward to the earth, calling it to witness that he now had the right to become the Enlightened One, and the earth responded with a thunderous roar.

This moment of enlightenment is described in *The Life of the Buddha,* one of the early Buddhist scriptures: "When the morning star appeared in the Eastern sky, the struggle was over and the prince's mind was as clear as the daybreak. It was December 8, when he was thirty-five years of age, that the prince became Buddha."

The Later Years

What had happened? The seeker had overcome the temptations of Mara, and had completed his quest, finding at last the answer to human suffering. Buddha means the enlightened one, and henceforth he is so called. What his thoughts were, and how he arrived at them, we shall describe later. Now, for the sake of continuity, we will continue his story.

A small group of traveling merchants came upon him, brought him food, and accompanied him to Benares. In a deer park close by, he preached his first sermon, "Setting in Motion the Wheel of the Law." He described the Middle Way, and other fundamental doctrines. Soon he was joined by the ascetics with whom he had spent six years of austerity. They were quick to recognize what he had achieved. As he wandered, he was joined by his father, wife, and son, whom he hadn't seen for many years. His son joined his order, and so did thousands of others. For forty-five years he preached his teachings in the Ganges valley, his followers being hosted and fed by wealthy disciples. Thus he continued until he was eighty years of age.

The place of his death was Kusinara. He had eaten some "soft pig food," which had given him stomach pains. Knowing his end was imminent, he lay down on his right side, his hand supporting his head. This, again, is a classic pose of the Buddha, known as the reclining Buddha. But more important than the scene of his passing are his last words. They are, "Strive with diligence, and be a lamp unto yourselves." In a sense, they set the tone for his entire teaching.

On U.S. Highway 1, a few miles south of the University of Miami, is a plant nursery. I enjoy driving by there because they always have on their sign a humorous saying or anecdote. Recently, it read, "If you are seeking a helping hand, look at the end of your arm." This is not only a clever saying, but it is pure Buddhism as well. The Buddha, who was reputed to have a sense of humor, would have enjoyed it, since it echoes his last words. "Be a lamp unto yourselves" means that if we are to gain insight and spiritual understanding, we must do it ourselves. Contrary to Western theology, there is no savior or god to pray to who will do it for us. There are no miraculous events to bring about our salvation. We must roll up our sleeves, and get to it ourselves. "Strive with diligence" means just what it says. It may not come easily, but keep working at it. And what does the Buddha do? As we said before, he is a guide, standing along the side of the path, pointing the way. To quote again from the ancient teachings: "The Buddha does but point the way."

And so, we come to the heart of the Buddha's teaching, which is actually what occurred under the Bo tree.

The Four Noble Truths

The heart of Buddhism lies in the Four Noble Truths. If we recall what was said earlier about Greek contributions to the West, we know that their development of logical reasoning is a cornerstone of our culture today. The syllogism, a means of arriving at a valid conclusion, is based on the concept that if we know two facts to be true, we may deduce from them a third statement which will also be true. This is called deductive reasoning.

Upon first reading the Four Noble Truths, I was startled by their similarity to Greek syllogisms. I have discussed this similarity with logicians, including the head of the logic department of a major university, and they all agreed that the teachings of the Buddha are clear, and founded on rational principles.

We will use the names of the Noble Truths in the original Sanskrit, which is the cultural language of ancient India.

Dukkha is the first Noble Truth. It is translated as sorrow, suffering, unhappiness, or separation from the pleasant. It is common to all humans, although it varies in degree. There is another meaning as well—a sense of unfulfillment, or incompleteness. We all know persons who seem to possess every-thing that should lead to a life of happiness; health, material wealth and possessions, and the comforts of modern life are theirs, yet they are neither happy nor satisfied. There seems to be a hollowness within them, that nothing seems to fill. Taken in either sense, no one can deny dukkha; it appears to be a universal human condition.

Karma is the second Noble Truth. Although this word has become part of our language, its popular use as a synonym for fate differs from its original meaning. Karma, in the original sense, is something we are all familiar with, and is a basic premise in science: It is the law of cause and effect. Every event has a cause; things just don't happen spontaneously, out of the blue. One visual image we are all familiar with and that illustrates karma is that of a space vehicle at Cape Canaveral being launched. The huge blast of the ignited fuel envelopes the base of the rocket; this is the cause. The ship slowly rises toward the heavens; this is the effect. No ignition, no launch.

Universal causality is so evident all around us, that we take it for granted. I sometimes illustrate the principle by holding a piece of chalk in the air. Although we can't see it, gravity is a cause affecting all of us. As I release the chalk, it doesn't fly upwards or sideways; it falls down. Gravity is the cause; the falling down of the chalk is the effect. So karma, the principle of cause and effect, is our second accepted truth.

The reasoning that follows in the Buddha's logic is, for me, one of the most beautiful and simple applications of rational thought to be found.

Drsta is the third Noble Truth. Here we must perform a basic logical procedure. If, as we have shown in the first Noble Truth, there is unhappiness in the world (dukkha), and if the law of cause and effect pertains (karma), then it must follow that if we remove the cause of the unhappiness, then by the law of karma, the unhappiness will disappear. If the fuel does not ignite, the space vehicle will not lift off. If there were no gravity acting on the chalk, it would fly to the ceiling. If whatever causes the dukkha is diminished or eliminated, the dukkha will be reduced or eliminated. Pure, simple logic.

This brings us to the most important question of all: What is this cause that we must destroy? The answer is Drsta, the third Noble Truth, and a word that I cannot pronounce. A key lies in the spelling however, for it is the base from which we derive the English word thirst.

Thirst means desire, craving, wanting things. It may also be expressed as attachment. We get attached to things, and to ideas as well.

We may know a married couple whose goal as parents is to have their child become a doctor. Everything is planned towards this end. But one day, they are told that after a few years of college, their child decides that his real interest is art, and he intends to pursue that as a career. The choice is devastating to the parents; they had become attached to the idea of his becoming a doctor.

We will expand on the concept of desire and attachments shortly, but let us return to the Noble Truths. The first part of the third truth is logically correct, that is, if everything has a cause, and if we remove the cause of unhappiness, we will end the unhappiness as well. But the second part, that the cause of suffering is desire, or wanting, is not proven at all. How do we know that the Buddha is right in his conclusion, that desire is the cause of our problems? We don't.

It is here that the Buddha's attitude comes forth: "Try it, and see if it works." This is a remarkably pragmatic view. And the best part is that we are our own judge. We are in a position to experiment with the concept. If we try to reduce our attachment to things and ideas, and find thereby that we sense an increased serenity or lessened anxiety, then it is working. However, if we see no worthwhile change, we can return to our previous ways. The Buddha emphasized here that he was not a divinity to be followed blindly; rather, he was a teacher offering a new outlook on life. Whether we used it was up to us.

As we approach the fourth Noble Truth, let us go back to a term that the Buddha sometimes used to describe himself— that is, a doctor. The physician performs only two functions. The first is to diagnose. He analyses the symptoms and comes to a conclusion as to the nature of the illness. The second duty is to treat the illness. It may require medication, or surgery, or rest. First the diagnosis, and then the treatment.

In the Four Noble Truths, the Buddha does just that. The first three, dukkha, karma, and drsta form the diagnosis. The illness is human unhappiness and the cause is desire and attachment. The fourth Noble Truth is the prescription, or treatment. It is called the Eightfold Path.

The Eightfold Path is the way in which the Buddha, similar to a doctor, finds the path to recovery for the patient. A manner of lifestyle is described, covering all aspects of life from deep personal commitment to interpersonal conduct and behavior. Divided into eight segments, the Path is as follows:

Right View
Right Intention
Right Speech
Right Action
Right Livelihood
Right Effort
Right Mindfulness
Right Concentration

The first two terms express the idea of intention. We should have an overall grasp of what we are trying to achieve, and a determination to do so. The next three are concerned with moral conduct. They describe how we should behave in business, communication with others, and such things as charitable deeds and community obligations. The final three emphasize the importance of concentration. It requires work and effort to achieve our goal. But what is our goal?

It is not within the scope of this book to elaborate or go into detail regarding the Eightfold Path, since in itself it is an extensive subject, covering most of the Buddhist teachings. What we will do, however, is to define our goal, and proceed toward it.

Nirvana

Let us consider theoretically the situation of a person who followed the Buddha's path to divest himself of all attachments and desires. The result is a state of what is referred to as enlightenment. Nirvana simply is another word for enlightenment. It literally means "blown out," a state in which the fires of desire, greed, lust, and craving are extinguished. What is left is a being free from all anxiety, doubt, fear, and unhappiness. The hollowness we described earlier is gone, and is replaced with inner serenity and tranquility.

But we don't need such exotic words as nirvana or enlightenment. Understanding is a valid synonym. One who begins to understand himself and his relationship with the world is in his own way enlightened. There is no outward change in such a person; they go about their daily activities in a normal manner. If anything, work and relationships are improved, since as anxieties and tensions are reduced, we can concentrate better on more productive endeavors.

Buddhism in Everyday Life

Making It Work

A few years ago, as my wife and I were nearing a Zen monastery in Japan, we paused for a few minutes as a line of monks passed us. Shaved heads, saffron robes, meditative expressions, and measured steps . . . the solemn procession was truly impressive. But as the file neared its end, we were startled to hear, in an unmistakable American accent, "How ya doin?" It was one of the last few monks in the line, and when we had the opportunity to speak with him, he told us about himself. A recent graduate of the Massachusetts Institute of Technology, he was an engineer. His family was from New England; his father, in the same profession, had held a place open for him in the firm.

But rather than enter the real world at that time, he chose to relinquish material gains to fulfill a personal need within himself. I sometimes wonder if he returned to his career after he completed his Zen training (which we will discuss later).

Few, if any, of us will discard our way of life and don the

saffron robes and begging bowl of a monk. We live in late twentieth century America, and follow a different path. To do this, we must modify the Buddhist concepts slightly.

A word must be added to the concept of attachments, and that word is "unnecessary." Certain attachments are too valuable to discard. Obviously, our loved ones—parents, children, spouses, family members, lovers, and dear friends—are in this group. Our home, our work, our favorite interests—these are not to be discarded. But once we get through the main list, we come upon a large grouping of things and ideas whose values are more nebulous. Do we really need them?

We in America are fed many myths. The three most damaging are that we may achieve happiness by being beautiful, or acquiring wealth, or by becoming famous. Bombarding us daily are commercials showing how a beauty cream or pair of jeans will make a girl more attractive, which in turn will make her life happier. A young man is told that a newer, more expensive car will make him attractive to women.

Wealth and fame are also touted as guarantees for happiness. "If I only had a million dollars, I'd really be happy for the rest of my life." "If I could be famous like Madonna, I'd never want anything else."

To any person who tells you this, you need only reply with two names: Elvis Presley, and Marilyn Monroe. Elvis' profile could have graced a Greek coin, and Marilyn's beauty is to this day world renowned. Both of them had more money than they could spend in a lifetime, and their fame continues years after their deaths. Yet both died miserably, prematurely and, reputedly, by their own hand. So much for the myths of beauty, fame and wealth.

This is not to say there is anything wrong with these things. I would most certainly prefer to have wealth than to be poor. And I would rather be attractive than ugly. For some people, fame may be a choice as well. What is wrong is to believe that these qualities are a guarantee of happiness and to be attached to them. It is not wrong to set a goal or work toward something, but it is wrong to let your happiness depend on whether you acquire it.

There are many illustrations of this kind of thinking. A very wealthy businessman, who was a devout Buddhist, had his own private Lear jet. When asked why a Buddhist would possess such a symbol of wealth, his reply was: "The jet is very convenient for me, and I enjoy using it. However, I was happy when I was poor and didn't have it, and should I be compelled through circumstance not to have it any longer, I would still be happy." In other words, his happiness did not depend on the jet; he was not attached to it.

I recently saw a very funny and successful comedian being interviewed on television. When he told the hostess of the show that he made more than $50 million in the last year, her next question was, "That must make you feel very good, doesn't it?" His answer revealed his intelligence: "It does, but not really that much. All the people follow me around, and I no longer know who are my friends and who are hanging on for the money and the glamour. My daily life hasn't changed that much, except that I work harder."

But the examples that mean the most are the ones I see personally. I gave some talks at Homestead Air Force Base a few years ago to airmen who had returned to the United States with wives from Japan, Korea, and other Asian countries. Buddhist wives and Christian or Jewish husbands sometimes had difficulty understanding the other's religion, and my lectures were designed to close the gaps.

I had spoken of how desire, or wanting, can lead to unhappiness. The following week, a young girl of about fourteen years of age raised her hand to tell a story. She had been walking with some friends through a mall, enjoying herself in their company. She passed a jewelry store and saw a watch in the window that she immediately liked, but its price placed it beyond her means. When she caught up with her group, her usually cheerful attitude had been replaced by glum disappointment. But then, she said, "I remembered what you said about wanting things, and how not being able to get them would make you sad. So I put the watch out of my mind, and was happy again!" A simple, pragmatic use of the knowledge she had acquired. Perhaps, being so young, her mind was open to new ideas.

Americans have had a love affair with the automobile for

decades. Much more than a means of transportation, the car may represent success, affluence, freedom in its mobility, a sense of power, and other emotional attachments as well.

Let us imagine we own a beautiful new automobile. Shining chrome, polished metal, space-age dashboard, and lots of horsepower. We really love this car! Suppose we park it in a supermarket lot, do our shopping, and upon returning to the car we find a sizeable dent in the door, with the paint cracked off. Our immediate reaction is a sick-to-the-stomach anger at what someone did to our beautiful automobile. This is terrible!

Now let us imagine the same scene, but with one exception. Same beautiful, well-polished car, same damage to it; but what differs here is our attitude toward the car. Yes, it's a great car and, yes, we enjoy it, but it is, after all, only an object made of steel, glass, and rubber, merely a means of transportation. Two days in the shop and it will be as good as new. We are still upset, but not nearly as much as in the first description of the occurrence.

What has changed? In the first example, we are very much attached to the car, and the mental and physiological response shows it. In the second example, our attachment is much less and, consequently, the response is diminished, certainly to our benefit. The pain we feel is in direct proportion to our attachment to the automobile. If we are fortunate enough to diminish our attachments to such things, then we begin to develop an inner tranquility that will serve us well in such unhappy episodes.

It becomes, therefore, a mental exercise in which we begin to develop a sense of what is *really* important to us, and to begin to distance ourselves from things or ideas that are of less consequence. This doesn't mean that we should give up anything we like or enjoy. It just means that we should not let our happiness depend on having it.

Attachment and Performance

Most of us have some kind of responsibilities of a business or professional, civic, social, or family nature. How does a change in our thinking affect such activities?

One way of expressing nonattachment is by looking at things objectively. One of the best examples is a physician. We all know that doctors generally will not treat their own family's illnesses or perform surgery on a family member. The reason is, of course, that they are emotionally involved, and this might influence their diagnostic or surgical skills. For most conditions other than a cold or minor illness, another doctor is brought in because he will treat the patient in a compassionate but emotionally uninvolved way.

This necessary objectivity pertains in the world of business as well. There is nothing wrong with a young person setting a goal to become a millionaire. But if that goal is pursued with an emotional blindness to everything else, then the objectivity and the ability to make rational decisions is lost. How many people have watched their favorite stock slowly go down the drain because they liked the stock, even though there were indications of its weakness?

We may watch two boxers of approximately equal skill and ability face off. But if one is an angry street slugger and the other a cool, nonemotional fighter waiting for an opening, we know on whom to bet.

This concept, carried to an extreme, is illustrated in a story about a Japanese Samurai warrior. His master had been slain, and it was the Samurai's duty to pursue the killer and avenge his master. After more than a year he found him, and drew his sword for the final act. At that moment, the murderer faced the warrior and spit in his face. At this, the warrior sheathed his sword and left.

Why? What had happened to prevent the warrior from avenging his master's murder?

As we shall see in the chapter on Zen Buddhism, Samurai, who are trained in the Zen Buddhist tradition, have learned to do their duty in a completely nonemotional, totally objective manner. When the killer spit in his face, the Samurai felt anger. Had he completed the act, it would have been tainted and shamed, since he would have been acting in part from his personal indignation, rather than from his impersonal sense of duty.

A final thought should be added at this point. Shedding our unnecessary attachments will not cause us to become cold, objective, and uninvolved. In fact, the opposite is true.

If we are trying to become less needlessly attached and to reduce our wanting and desiring, then we are gradually approaching a state of understanding or enlightenment. There are two sides to the coin of enlightenment: wisdom, and compassion. If we are able to realize that some things we considered so important to our happiness are really not so important after all, then we are truly acquiring wisdom. And with that wisdom comes a sense of serenity and inner peace. But furthermore, a sense of compassion develops simultaneously, since the inner peace reduces the hostility and anxiety, and we face the world differently. Compassion is discussed later in this chapter.

Buddhist Imagery

One question in particular is often asked by people newly introduced to Buddhism. If the Buddha was human, and if there are no gods in the Buddhist philosophy—religion, then why do we always see people praying to and worshipping statues of the Buddha? There are two answers to this question.

Strictly speaking, when you approach a statue or painting of the Buddha, what you see is an image representing a human being who, through his perseverance, effort, and intuition was able to uncover the cause of human suffering. Furthermore, he devoted the rest of his life to teaching his findings to others. The message to the viewer is that he, a human like the rest of us, was able to find inner peace; so may we, by his example, follow the same path. This is the Buddhist belief.

The other reason is that, as the centuries passed and Buddhism became institutionalized, many changes occurred. Until this point, we have been discussing the historical Buddha. But as Buddhism spread to other countries, it encountered peoples with already established religions and gods. The simple truth is, most religions have gods and people expect them. Contrary to the Christian religion, which has attempted to eradicate and destroy the religions and gods of any country into which it was introduced, Buddhism is tolerant of all religions, and does not attempt to replace them. Therefore, the Buddha was made into a god in addition to the ones already present, or became manifestations of existent gods. There are innumerable sects of Buddhism, combining all sorts of other gods, divine beings, heavenly saints and angels, and various minor deities as well. As I said earlier, we have been studying the historical Buddha and his teachings. What happened to Buddhism in later years is fascinating and enjoyable reading, but because it is so filled with mystical and esoteric beliefs, it is beyond the scope of this book.

By far and away, what strikes us first when we approach an

image of the Buddha, is the facial expression and body pose. The serenity, tranquility, and inward composure all represent his nirvana. The inner peace that has replaced all anxiety, tension, and suffering shows with the half closed eyes and suggestion of a smile. This is truly the "peace that surpasseth all understanding," which to me is the outstanding achievement of Buddhist art.

The Buddha may be represented in four body poses: sitting in the lotus (meditative) position, which represents his becoming enlightened under the bo tree; the standing position, which represents his teaching; the walking pose, which represents his forty-five years of spreading his knowledge to his early disciples; and his reclining position, lying on his right side with his hand supporting his head, which illustrates his departure from life. Images in any other position, such as sitting in a relaxed pose, are not images of the Buddha.

There are certain other characteristics relating to the Buddha's image. Long ear lobes are subject to two interpretations; they represent the wisdom that was acquired through his enlightenment, and they also remind us that he was a prince before he became enlightened. In those days princes in India wore heavy gold earrings, and the result, as anyone who wears them will tell you, is elongated earlobes.

We often find a raised small bump or a mark in the center of the forehead. This, too, is subject to multiple interpretations. It may illustrate the opening of the "third eye," which means the acquiring of the wisdom of enlightenment, or it may represent the small tuft of white hair that the Buddha had there, one of his several physical attributes.

Deserving of special attention are the positions of his hands, which are called mudras. These have a special place in Buddhistic imagery, and there are books with scores, if not hundreds of them, illustrated. We already know the position of the right hand pointing downward, which calls on the earth to witness his enlightenment. Another well-known mudra is that of the palm of the hand facing outward towards the viewer, which is known as the protective mudra. I once purchased a Burmese Mandalay Buddha, in the standing position, with the right hand hanging straight down, holding a round object between the thumb and middle finger, with the palm facing outwards. I couldn't find this position illustrated in any of my reference books, and was sure that it represented some obscure, subtle concept. Months later, while visiting New York, I finally found a book that contained an explanation of this imagery. The Buddha was doing nothing more exotic than holding a piece of fruit!

Most effective, however, in portraying the value that the ideas of this philosophy can have upon our daily lives is the seat upon which the Buddha sits. This is frequently the lotus flower, which has a special meaning because of its unusual nature. The lotus floats on the filthiest of waters, and yet is untouched by the foulness of its surroundings. It maintains a serene beauty of its own, close to yet at the same time apart from that from which it springs.

This portrayal of the lotus applies directly and beautifully to one who has acquired enlightened understanding. Surrounded by the rudeness, tensions, travails, and what Shakespeare refers to in *Hamlet,* act 3, as the "insolence of office" that one may be exposed to on almost a daily basis, it is yet possible to maintain a serenity and detachment that insulates us from our unpleasant surroundings, just as the lotus floats calmly on the most polluted waters.

There are many excellent books available that illustrate in great detail the techniques, styles, colors, and unending variations characteristic of Buddhistic art. What lies within the scope of this book, however, is the general aura that emanates from good imagery of the Buddha, that quality of inward peace and inner strength that enables one to confront the problems of the day.

To round out our knowledge of Buddhism, and thereby enhance our ability to avail ourselves of the wisdom we wish to acquire from it, we should have some understanding of two of the concepts that evolved in Buddhism. (A third, and the most important and useful outgrowth, Zen Buddhism, is discussed in the next chapter.)

The Bodhisattva

A bodhisattva is one who has personally achieved all the requirements for nirvana, but rather than enter the final stage, chooses instead to help others acquire it.

Imagine a college graduation ceremony. Faculty and graduating seniors are wearing their caps and gowns. As their names are called off, the line of students leading to the dean's podium moves slowly forward, and each student is handed his diploma.

One student in the line, however, looks down into the audience and sees a few of his classmates who are not graduating. Perhaps they have not completed their requirements, or have not passed their examinations. He makes an important decision at this point. Rather than graduate, he chooses to remain in the school and assist his friends with their work, so they may all graduate together at a future time.

Let us now change the scene. Imagine a mountain whose top is nirvana. Most of us are at the bottom of this mountain, slowly climbing up toward our enlightenment. Some travelers are nearing the top. Very near the goal, however, is one person who has overcome all the difficulties and is ready to reap the rewards of his struggles. He looks backward, however, and sees the long line of those struggling up the path behind him. He makes the same decision as the graduating student: Rather than take the final step into nirvana, he elects to go back to help all those who still struggle, vowing to assist everyone who needs it, so all may become enlightened together.

Only one word describes such an act, and that word is compassion. One who would give up his or her final stage of enlightenment to be able to help others is, in Buddhist thought, the highest personification of this virtue. To quote from the texts: "I must lead all sentient beings into liberation, and will stay here until the end, even if it is for one living soul!"

Bodhisattvas are elegantly portrayed in Buddhist iconology. They look very much like the Buddha, but with a major difference. The Buddha's hair is normally represented by small, spiral curls. But the headdress of a bodhisattva is a crown. Before the Buddha became enlightened, he was a prince, who wore a prince's crown; therefore, a bodhisattva, who is destined to become enlightened in the future, wears a crown. The "snail curl" is found only on Buddha images. Furthermore, bodhisattvas may be pictured in a relaxed leaning position, often with the legs partly outstretched; such informal poses are never used for the Buddha.

Bodhisattvas may be male or female. The most popular is the "Kuan Yin" in China; known as "Kannon" in Japan. She is referred to as the Goddess of Compassion, to whom families pray for good fortune, especially for such events as birth, graduation, and marriage. She is beautifully portrayed as a lovely woman with an exquisite headdress, often carrying symbolic images of charity and good will.

The two major male bodhisattvas are Maitraya, the Buddha who is yet to come, and Manjusri, the manifestation of wisdom and knowledge. The mythology of the many bodhisattvas is extensive and elaborate, but they all represent the wisdom and compassion that is the essence of the religion itself.

Samsara

If nirvana is the state of enlightenment, wherein we are free from our wants and desires, and the fires of passion are extinguished, what is the opposite of this condition?

The answer is samsara. This word is used to express our daily existence, with its ups and downs, pains and pleasures, frustrations and joys. Thoreau, when he wrote that most people lead lives of quiet desperation, could well have been describing samsara. As we noted earlier, many people who seem to have everything are unsatisfied with their lives, and constantly seek for something that is missing. The problem is that they are not quite sure just what that is.

The main effort in Buddhism, therefore, is to transcend from samsara to nirvana. This gradual transition, this path that one may follow, has been laid out in the Buddha's teachings. He first established the cause of our being locked into samsara, and then showed us the way out. The Buddha described himself as a guide who but points the way, encouraging us to give it a try. If it makes our daily lives better, then we have lost nothing and gained much.

Visualize once again the mountain, with Nirvana at the top, and those seeking a release from stress and anxiety near the bottom, gradually winding their way upwards toward a more fulfilling life.

What if someone were to come along and show us a way to reach the top in a split second? Imagine being able to transcend samsara and reach nirvana in less time than it takes to read this sentence!

This is exactly what happened, and what can be done. It is called Zen.

4

The Sound of One Hand Clapping

The finger pointing at the moon is not the moon.
—*BODHIDARMA (ZEN) SAYING*

THE CONCEPT OF acquiring insight or enlightenment in a split second astounds the imagination. How can this be done?

To illustrate this idea, let's listen to a dialogue using the Socratic method. (Socrates felt that the student often has the answer deep within himself, and a good teacher is able to draw it out by asking the right questions.)

Before leaving for class that morning, the professor picked four or five camellias from the garden, and placed them in a paper bag.

Professor: The answer to the question of how one attains sudden en-
lightenment is inside this bag.

Taking the flowers from the bag and holding them up to the class, the professor then asks:

Professor: Are these flowers beautiful?
Class (almost in unison, and without hesitation): Yes!
Professor: Do you need me to tell you that they are beautiful?
Class: No!
Professor: In other words, even if I were out of the room, you would
still know these flowers are beautiful.
Class: Yes!
Professor: Suppose I were to begin to dissect the flower, and name each
part—petal, stem, pistil, stamen, etc. Would this make the flower
more beautiful?
Class: No.
Professor: Last question. How do you know that these flowers are
beautiful?

There is a pause, followed by various answers from the class. (If in a minute or so the correct answer is not given, the professor will say:)

Professor: It is something that women are especially good at.
Class: Intuition!

And they are right! Zen, or sudden enlightenment, comes to us through intuition. The question asking whether they needed the professor to tell them the flowers are beautiful points out that they know this within themselves. The next question, which concerns dissecting and naming the various parts of the flower, represents the Western way of analysis. The original beauty of the flower is there to be grasped instantly. We don't need to discuss it or analyze it. It's just there.

To summarize: Traditional Buddhism follows a path of gradual enlightenment, whereas Zen Buddhism seeks sudden enlightenment. The goal is the same—understanding, nirvana, enlightenment, insight into reality. "There are many paths leading to the top of the mountain, but they all arrive at the same place."

I cannot arrive at this point without thinking of a similar concept in a totally different setting: classical music.

The great symphonies written about two hundred years ago are considered by most to be the finest in Western history, and the two composers most noted are Beethoven and Mozart. A difference, however, lies in their methods. Beethoven's works each took from eighteen months to two years to write, and the manuscripts are filled with changes, erasures, additions, and corrections. The final creations, however, are unsurpassed in their majesty; they represent a God-given genius, painstakingly hard work, and endless effort, all superimposed upon the terrible handicap of increasing deafness.

By contrast, Mozart's works were usually completed in a matter of weeks. Amazingly, most of his manuscripts are without one erasure or change! He wrote them down already finished. Even Salieri, one of Mozart's greatest rivals, praised his work, saying that "One more note would be superfluous; one less note, and something would be missing." In other words, they were perfect!

Mozart, too, had a God-given genius, intensive training, and a tremendous drive to work. But he had something else, as well—an amazing intuitive ability wherein the music seemed to spring fully developed from his mind. The completed works of these two masters are some of the finest music ever written; but their methods were entirely different.

And so it is with Buddhism. For some people, the traditional step-by-step approach works well. For others, perhaps those more intuitive by nature, the sudden method is a good choice. It is the purpose of this chapter to become familiar with Zen. Then both options will be open to us, and still following our pragmatic heritage, we may see which works better for us.

Background to Zen Study

Many who teach about Zen feel that someone who has been raised exclusively with a Western background is able to make a cold leap into Zen. I disagree.

It is almost an impossible task to jump into this kind of study without a gradual and prior introduction to the workings of the Far Eastern mind. We have now come to this point.

First, we learned where we came from. We discussed our ways of thinking and approaching the world based upon our Greek heritage and values, our Judeo-Christian inheritance, and the American notion of pragmatism.

We then introduced Taoism, a basic Far Eastern concept of an underlying, all-encompassing cosmos, where living in harmony creates a deep inner serenity.

Next, we met the historical Buddha, and found that his rational evaluation of the cause and the cure for human unhappiness can be of benefit to us.

We now have sufficient insight into the Eastern way of looking at life to take the next step. And a giant step it is! But it will be a gradual and rational approach, as opposed to a sudden plunge from one culture into another of a totally different nature.

"Beat" Zen

A major setback for the introduction of Zen into the United States was that it occurred in California in the late 1950s, the same place and time that the beat generation was taking hold.

Being antiestablishment in nature, the beat movement

(which was later to evolve into the flower-child and hippie period) adapted one aspect of Zen which seemed, to them, perfectly suited to it.

We have already learned that intuition is the driving force in the Zen approach to enlightenment. This means that it does not depend on reason, rationality or logic; in fact, intellect is sometimes a barrier to insight. Zen often appears to be irrational and unintellectual and, therefore, somewhat erratic. This superficial aspect appealed to the beat movement, which adapted it to its own use and erroneously supposed Zen Buddhism to be totally compatible with their antiestablishment movement.

Nothing could be further from the truth. Zen is a flowering of the original, traditional Buddhism, and has behind it fifteen hundred years of enrichment by generations of masters whose wisdom and insight rival those of our Western culture. The distorted image projected by the beat Zen group blurred the true picture. Learning how Zen evolved from traditional Buddhism will clarify its unique status.

Setting the Stage

An understanding of the cultural and religious climate that existed in China at the time is necessary before we proceed. Illustrative anecdotes and historical comparisons are of value here, as they show how institutionalizing a religion affects its growth.

A prince once lived in Persia; at the age of twenty-one, he married a beautiful princess. For one year they lived a life of perfect bliss, and then she died. The prince mourned grievously, and had her body placed in a silver casket.

A short time later, he decided to put the casket in a small garden and surround it with roses. Not long after that, he thought a small pond would enhance the setting. Still later, several trees were added, and so on. Two years later he sat gazing at several acres of lakes with swans, elaborate flower gardens, elegant tree arrangements, and beautiful terraces. In the center of it all lay the silver casket.

After contemplating the scene for an hour, the prince said, "Only one thing is spoiling this." Pointing to the silver casket, he ordered his servant to remove it.

The message of this story is obvious and, unfortunately, it pertains to most religions. The original ideas, usually clear and unpretentious, become so enmeshed in endless ritual and organized splendor that the true meaning of the religion is lost.

In eighteenth century Russia, Jewish culture was highly scholastic and intellectual. The common working man, uneducated and often illiterate, felt left out of his religion. A leader known as the Bal Shem Tov arose, who asked where the original concept of Jewish theology had gone. Had not Abraham, the patriarch, conversed with God's angel? Judaism meant more than just sitting around the table studying the ancient scrolls, an activity reserved for scholars alone. It was a simple and joyous relationship between man and God, available to any Jew, rich or poor, learned or not. This was the reaction to an overly ritualized and academic approach to Judaism. Those who joined this movement led by the Bal Shem Tov became known as the Hasidim. They became a powerful religious entity within Judaism, and exist to this day.

Within Christianity, similar reactions have occurred. In 1517 Martin Luther reached a point where he could no longer tolerate the corruption and some of the teachings of the Catholic Church at that time. When he nailed his "95 theses" to the door of his church, he was objecting to what the religion had become as compared with what it was originally.

And in the Far East, at the beginning of the sixth century, something similar was occurring. Buddhism had originated in India about 500 B.C. By the time of Christ, it had been carried to China by priests and merchants via the great trade routes.

Five hundred years later, it was firmly entrenched in China. The great Emperor Wu had fervently embraced Buddhism, and had spent much of the royal treasury building monasteries and libraries, and subsidizing and encouraging the religious endeavors of the priests. The populace itself was in a sort of religious fervor, and huge caves containing thousands of carved images of Buddhas and bodhisattvas were carved out of solid rock.

But someone was about to appear who would advance the practice of Buddhism and break free from traditional ritualization. His name was Bodhidarma, and he was the first patriarch of Zen.

Zen Buddhism

Before taking our first step, this is the time to recall the Zen story about the teacup. Master Nan-in compared the professor's head to a teacup, already so full that it would hold no more. We should now be ready to empty a few drops of tea from the "cup" in our heads, and make room for some fresh ideas from Zen, which is considered by many to be a jewel of Eastern wisdom. Although Zen may seem remote from our traditional Western mentality, the attempt to understand it is worth the effort.

The barrier that confronts us is the use of intuition. As we illustrated earlier in this chapter, Zen relies on our ability to acquire insight by using our intuition. Almost all Western philosophy opposes this, and we have been led to believe that basic truths can be arrived at through logic and reason, that rational thought alone points the way. Plato, Spinoza, Locke, and Kant refer to intuitive processes in their writings, but not as major factors in identifying truth; the thrust of Western philosophy is away from intuition and toward pure reason.

Reflective, rational thought is one of mankind's greatest gifts. Once systematized by the Greek thinkers, and then refined and expanded through our modern Western philosophers, it is a major source of our political and technical advances. The entire world is a beneficiary of the scientific method, which through medicine and technology have advanced us beyond the dreams of our ancestors.

Yet intuition must be given its just due. Einstein's remarkable theories, since proven, were the result of sudden insights into problems he had worked on for years. The glimpse of a genius who grasps a fundamental truth does not come out of the blue. It springs forth from a mind that has dwelt on the question previously. Newton, Freud, and Darwin are only a small part of a long list of individuals whose genius, hard work, and insight have enriched us beyond measure.

As we begin our study of Zen, we should be prepared for some "non-sense." This does not mean "nonsense," that is, "stupid," or "silly." What it does mean is knowledge that is acquired not through reason or intellect but through insight. All the logic in the world will not prove that a rose is beautiful, but we know it instantly.

The word Zen is a Japanese translation of the Chinese word Ch'an, which in turn derives from the Sanskrit Dhyana, which means meditation. Zen acquired its name from the belief that deep meditation is one means of gaining sudden insight.

In about the year 520 A.D., Bodhidarma traveled from India to China. He was the twenty-eighth patriarch (i.e., spiritual leader) of Indian Buddhism. What he saw in China we have already learned—tremendous Buddhist activity among monks and laity alike, sponsored by the enthusiasm of Emperor Wu, who had embraced the religion totally.

But he also realized that the intensity was directed toward temples and images, ritual and ceremony, which seemed to him a far cry from the original teachings of the Buddha. A thousand years had passed since the Buddha had lived, and it seemed to Bodhidarma that the true meaning of Buddhism had slipped away.

He felt that it was time to get back to basics. Since the message of the Buddha was to seek insight or enlightenment, Bodhidarma founded a form of the religion that was simplicity itself. There is no better way to express it than as a direct quotation:

A special transmission outside the Scriptures;
No dependence upon words or letters;
Direct pointing to the heart of man;
Seeing into one's own nature.

This means that we should not rely on any words at all, either in written or spoken form. The insight is within ourselves, not in any lectures or books; we must look into our own hearts, for that is where the answer lies. This is what Zen is all about, quoted directly from its founder, the first patriarch.

What it means to us from a practical standpoint is that Zen cannot be taught, but it can be transmitted. If anyone ever says that they can teach you Zen, whether in a book or vocally, they are not telling the truth. It *cannot* be taught.

This brings us to one of the most remarkable intellectual challenges ever faced: How do you teach that which cannot be taught? How has Zen been handed down for fifteen hundred years, generation to generation, by transmitting but not teaching it? And why is it that any attempt to teach Zen is useless?

"The Finger Pointing at the Moon Is Not the Moon"

The statement above was Bodhidarma's reaction to how he saw Buddhism being practiced in China. It ranks with the highest truisms of any culture.

The moon represents the goal or end result, which is gaining insight. The finger-pointing is the method or means used to do so. If someone is pointing to the moon, we should look at the moon. If we concentrate on the finger, we will never see that celestial disc. And so it is in religions. If we become totally involved with the ritual, we lose sight of the original meaning.

This is why teaching Zen is useless. Words, scriptures, discussions, and imagery entrap the Zen student in a maze and divert his attention from what was originally being sought.

But there is a larger interpretation of the moon analogy, which pertains to our daily lives. In any effort we make, for whatever goal we choose, we should not become sidetracked by multiple diversions which block out our ultimate objective. In this world of endless options and divergent views, it is important to cut through unnecessary distractions and focus on the goal. This is where intuition lends us its inherent benefit.

And, in one sense, this is what is done in a Zen monastery. It is an institution dedicated to increasing intuitive abilities. To my knowledge, there are no other centers of learning dedicated to this endeavor.

So we are back to the same question: How can we teach that which cannot be taught? Since the days of Bodhidarma, Zen masters have devised several ways to do just that. One of them is the koan.

The Koan

A koan is a sort of riddle or statement that cannot be answered by the intellect, and yet it must be answered. Perhaps the best known example is: "What is the sound of one hand clapping?" How do we answer this? We can summon all the Western reason and logic we have at our command, and it will be to no avail. We cannot go over, under, through, or around this question. Rational thought is paralyzed.

Nor can we answer it, as I have heard at times, with such replies as "the sound of silence." This is a frivolous answer, a word game.

In Zen monasteries the master, after interviewing the student monk and learning something about him, will assign him such a koan. The neophyte then begins to concentrate and meditate upon it, and may do so for weeks, months, or even years. He becomes increasingly frustrated, and builds up a "head of steam," a pressure, to solve it. The more intelligent and thoughtful he is, the harder it is for him to solve the koan, since these qualities do not help. His need to solve the koan is sometimes described as a "red hot ball of iron in his throat, which he can neither cough up nor swallow."

If, in the master's judgment, sufficient time has passed and no progress has been made, the monk may be given a new koan. But something else may happen. After much disappointment, frustration, and depression caused by trying and concentrating to the utmost, a stage of such desperation and tension builds up that something is ready to burst through.

It is said that a doctor who is a good diagnostician can make a preliminary diagnosis based on what he observes when the patient first enters the office. The gait, skin, posture, and other physical signs reveal to the trained eye some inkling of the condition.

And so it is with a Zen master. Through observation of and daily interviews with the monk, he can tell if the breakthrough is nearing or has already occurred. The monk's expression and manner of entrance into the master's room can reveal to the master the monk's condition.

If the master feels that the awakening is imminent, he can give the monk a final push to achieve it. Perhaps it is a certain statement or question. Frequently it may be physical; a blow from the master's staff may be what is needed. This is not intended to be cruel, but to give the student a shock that pushes him beyond his rational thought and into a new plane. A sharp blow can knock the nonsense out of the student monk, or perhaps knock some sense into him. Such acts may appear strange to our Western eyes, but given at the right time by an experienced master, they can produce the desired result.

There are about seventeen hundred koans that are used. One of my favorites is "Joshu's Mu."

Joshu, a Chinese Zen master who lived in the ninth century, was approached by a monk who asked, "Does a dog have Buddha nature or not?" Joshu answered "Mu!"

This koan is a double question: (1) Does a dog have Buddha nature? and (2) What did Joshu mean by "mu"? Mu literally means no thing, a negative expression; it does not mean nothing. The answer, as with all koans, avoids a logical response. I was fortunate to visit a monastery where this koan is used, and I purchased a calligraphy of this expression which now hangs in my study. When confronted with a problem that is confusing, with multiple potential ramifications, I look at "Joshu's Mu." Perhaps it is my imagination, but I feel that it removes the cobwebs from my thinking and cuts through the maze to the best solution.

> Some other koans are:
>
> What was your face like before your parents were born?
>
> A cow gave birth to a calf on top of a flagpole.
>
> A goose is inside a bottle. Get him out without killing the goose or breaking the bottle.

These are not nonsense; they are "non-sense," that is, they cannot be solved by sensible thought, but they must be confronted. But Western minds are logical and our intellect and reason make koans confusing. Once we overcome this barrier, our intuitive self, which is in fact our true inner nature, is freed to grasp the answer.

What happens when this breakthrough occurs will be discussed later in this chapter. For now, let us turn to other methods of gaining insight.

The Mondo

A mondo is a short anecdote, frequently a dialogue between a disciple and a master. It illustrates an important principle, but its meaning, like that of a koan, must be grasped intuitively. It cannot be explained.

This example illustrates how feminine insight may work to one's advantage: A female disciple, on her first day at a Zen monastery, visited the master for a short interview in the evening. As darkness fell, she requested permission to leave. The master gave her a lighted lantern to carry as she walked back to her cottage. Just as she was opening the door to leave, the master walked to her and blew out the lantern. At that moment, she was enlightened!

To this day, many Japanese businessmen, professionals, working people, and others will spend a weekend at a Zen monastery. This modern mondo illustrates how the Zen influence still endures.

On a Friday night, a Japanese businessman fell asleep on the train that was taking him to the monastery. He went past his stop, and by the time he arrived, it was quite late. The master was at the gate.

> Businessman: I'm sorry I'm late. I was very tired and fell asleep on the train.
>
> Master (touching the gatepost): Is this post tired?

The man could not answer, and went to his cottage to sleep. In the middle of the night, he awoke and the meaning of the question, as well as the answer, became apparent to him. He went to the master and woke him, saying, "Yes, the post is tired." By his manner and answer, he had revealed to the master that he had become enlightened.

Some other mondos:

Disciple: Master, I cannot pacify my soul!

Master: Bring me your soul, and I will pacify it for you.

Disciple (the following day): Master, I have been searching for my soul, but I cannot find it!

Master: Good! If you cannot find your soul, then it is already pacified!

Disciple: Master, tell me the meaning of Zen!

Master: Come back tomorrow at four o'clock and I will tell you.

Disciple (the following day): It is four o'clock, Master, and I am here.

Master: Come close to me that I may whisper the meaning to you.

The monk comes close to the master and leans forward. The master gives him a box on the ears.

Master: There! Now you know!

Nonsense? No. "Non-sense?" Yes. The meaning is there, but it must be reached through insight.

One of my favorites, and one that can be explained to some extent, is the following:

Disciple (For some reason, I always imagine this disciple as having a whiny, Woody Allen-type voice.): Master, why is it we have to get dressed every morning, and then go eat?

Master: We dress; we eat.

Disciple: But Master, I do not understand!

Master: If you don't understand, then go get dressed and eat your breakfast!

This apparently superficial dialogue leads us to one of the most basic doctrines, which in turn may be expressed in a two-line mondo, attributed to one of the great masters:

Disciple: Master, what is Zen?

Master: Zen is everyday life.

> *The student monk was unhappy with the daily routine. He was searching for some sort of release from his normal schedules, some kind of exhilarating change. Such is not the case. Zen life is everyday life. There is no other place to go. No guru awaits us at the top of a mountain to liberate us. There is no pot of gold at the end of the rainbow; no nirvana beckons us from a distance. It is all here and now.*

This does not mean that if we just go on with our ordinary life that sooner or later we will acquire a direct seeing into our own nature. As the Buddha said in his dying statement, "strive with diligence." He also said, at an earlier time in his life, referring to himself as a human, that "within this six feet lies the entire universe." What we seek is already within us, and therefore within our everyday lives. But if we already possess it, why are we not aware of it? We shall return to this question later.

Another question can now be answered. When confronted with these mind-wracking koans and mondos, why can't someone just teach us the solutions? The answer is that they are something like a joke; nobody can explain it to you. Consider this example:

Man (upon entering a restaurant): Do you serve crabs here?
Waiter: Certainly, sir; we serve anyone. Have a seat!

Now, either a person will get the joke, or not. If he does, he may chuckle. If not . . . well, we all know what happens when you try to explain a joke.

In the same way, it is not only useless to explain a koan or mondo, but it is detrimental to the student's progress. Either he grasps the meaning intuitively, by himself, or not at all.

So important is this concept, that the Zen writings tell of a famous master who received a new disciple. This young man was very intelligent, and had memorized the scriptures. The master also sensed an air of self satisfaction bordering on arrogance about the disciple. He therefore summoned the neophyte to his room and asked him the following simple question: "Where do we go when we die?" The scriptures raced through the mind of the disciple, but he could not provide a satisfactory answer.

He stayed up the entire night, searching through all the available writings, to no avail. By the next day, he had arrived at a high state of tension and frustration. Angrily approaching the master, he grabbed him by the throat exclaiming, "Tell me the answer, or I shall kill you." Despite repeated threats, the master laughed, saying, "If I won't give you the answer while I'm alive, you surely won't get it from me when I'm dead!" Suddenly the student was aware of what he done, and ran away from the monastery, vowing to do penance and live the life of a hermit for the rest of his life. After many years of humility and regret, he did achieve enlightenment.

The purpose of this narrative is to illustrate the unshakable commitment of the master; even when threatened with death, he would not jeopardize the student's path to insight by telling him the answer.

The Zen Monastery

Few of us will spend any time in a Zen monastery, but it is to our benefit to acquire some knowledge of its function.

The life within is spartan. The monks usually arise at 4 A.M. Food is sparse and simple, frequently not much more than rice and pickled vegetables. Rooms are cold, furniture and bedding uncomfortable.

The days are spent working and meditating. Work is the supreme virtue; the saying common to most Zen monasteries is, "No working, no eating." (This provides us with a clue regarding Japan's success today.) A monk may be assigned to gardening, working in the kitchen, and other activities designed to keep the school self-supporting.

Many hours are spent on mental and/or physical discipline, such as meditating upon an assigned koan, or learning to breathe in the correct way. Techniques vary with the monastery and the method of teaching used by the master.

However, a most unusual element—humor—is a part of the daily life. Much of this results from the attempts by the monks to trap one another into an intellectual quagmire. Hooking someone into a nonintuitive response becomes a sort of game. There are, therefore, two aspects of Zen Buddhism that are unique among the world's religions. To the best of my knowledge, humor and the deliberate cultivation of intuition appear nowhere else.

All these activities—the master–student relationship, the koans and mondos, the work, meditation, and self-discipline—are directed toward one goal: that split second of insight which will forever alter one's entire view of life.

Satori

Satori is the name given for the moment when the break-through occurs. It is the very first stage of seeing into one's own nature. A good master recognizes this in the neophyte monk, and it is referred to as "the end and the beginning." It is the end of the struggle to break through the bonds of rational thought and grasp, through intuition or insight, a new concept of life or reality as we know it. But it is also a first taste, the beginning of the exhilarating and exciting path seeking to enlarge and expand what has been acquired.

Actually, nothing has changed. Through intuitive awareness, only our perspective has been altered. We will return later to elaborate, but now it is time to turn our attention once again to our everyday Western lives.

5

Disciple: Master, What Is Zen?

Zen Master: Zen is Everyday Life!
—*A ZEN MONDO*

IHAVE HEARD many times that it is impossible for Zen to come West. It is claimed that we are so indoctrinated with Western culture that we simply cannot absorb any Far Eastern philosophies. I have also been told more than once that it is wrong to learn about these teachings for practical purposes, that it should be done for its spiritual value only. Furthermore, since there are so few Zen masters in the United States, it is claimed that the interested person simply cannot find anyone to instruct him.

I have found that one who is interested, and willing to make some personal effort, can certainly open their mind enough to absorb at least some of this learning. And if one wishes to do this for purely spiritual reasons, there is certainly nothing wrong with that; it is in fact a quality to be admired. But I have found in years of teaching that we are a pragmatic people, and love to not only learn something, but to put that knowledge to practical use in our everyday lives.

We have traced Zen from its beginning, and have learned some of the ways in which it is passed on to this day.

Since few of us will join a monastery and don the saffron robe, let us see what methods are available to us here and now to find a way to deeper insights.

Meditation

Meditation has many forms. Some center on correct breathing and concentrate on posture and positioning of the hands. Others use mantras, or chants. All these variations are means to an end.

Frequently, the one that is the least complicated is the one that works best. But before that method can be introduced, we should take one more look at exactly what our goal is in order to see how meditation will point us in the right direction.

Let's again picture ourselves following a path up the mountain where nirvana awaits us at the top. Keep in mind that there are many paths to the top of the mountain, and that they all lead to the same place. This is just one of those paths. We have gradually shed most of our unnecessary attachments, and are getting quite close to the summit. There looms before us one last barrier, or attachment, that we must overcome. With what do we identify so strongly that disassociation becomes almost impossible?

The answer is *ourselves!* Our attachment to the concept of self, the "I," the ego, is the final barrier. Once overcome, the pathway lies clear.

This is probably the most difficult concept to understand. "I" am here; "you" are there. We are faced once again with the basic difference between Western and Eastern thought: The Westerner *observes* the universe; the Easterner sees himself as an integral part of it.

But just what is this "I"? Great Western philosophers have delved deeply into this problem. One such philosopher, David Hume, in the eighteenth century, came to the conclusion that what we call the self is actually a bundle of different perceptions. To quote Hume: "When I enter most intimately into myself, I always stumble into one particular perception or another . . . I can never catch myself at any time without a perception."

The view generally accepted in the East, that one is a part

of the universe, has only been touched on by philosophers in the West. We need to begin to accept ourselves as part of a universe. How may we begin? Meditation is one effective way.

Our minds are continuously working, with thoughts coming and going, seemingly at will. The Buddha said that our minds are like a tree full of chattering monkeys, and it is this endless chattering that keeps us from seeing our real selves. We need to quiet our minds.

This is a wonderful mental exercise to try. Sit in a comfortable chair or on the floor. You can use the usual meditative positions of full lotus or half lotus, or just sit with your legs crossed. The room should be quiet. Close your eyes halfway. (Keeping them wide open will bring too many outside distractions, and closed eyes may encourage sleep.) Now try to think of nothing at all. It's impossible! All sorts of thoughts keep running through your mind. "What dress shall I wear tonight?" "What time do I tee off tomorrow?" "Is my shopping list complete?" "Where shall we have dinner?" Something is always there to occupy our thoughts.

There is no way to keep thoughts out of our minds. We must allow them to enter; we have no other choice. But once there, there is a way to handle them. Two techniques may work. We may envision ourselves lying on a grassy field, watching clouds drift into our view, and then drift away. Envision each thought that enters our minds as one of these clouds and let it lazily drift away. Another technique involves visualizing a stage with Fred Astaire in the center. Ginger Rogers enters from one of the wings, he spins her around a few times, and she then exits from the stage. In other words, accept the idea, "dance" with it for awhile, and then let it go. Each of us can create our own imaginative scenes to dissolve the thoughts as they appear, helping us to acquire an "empty" mind.

Whichever method you choose, it is important to persevere. We may begin with confidence, and later become discouraged as thoughts and ideas continue to emerge. But it becomes apparent that one can only think of certain things so many times before those thoughts begin to thin out.

It is at this point that our mind begins to empty or clear. As the endless parade of thoughts and ideas begins to fade, room is made for something else. This something else is not coming in from some outside source; it has been there all along. It is our own intuitive self, now becoming free to emerge. This spontaneous intuition is what links us to the universe, and diminishes our sense of apartness, which creates the feeling of isolation and loneliness.

The importance of what is happening lies in the realization that we cannot reason or intellectualize ourselves into acquiring this increased intuitive ability. In fact, intelligent, rational persons usually hinder themselves by trying to think their way into this kind of insight. Whether we follow the path of gradual enlightenment (traditional Buddhism) or the path of sudden enlightenment (Zen Buddhism), the process itself is intuitive. We just have to know it; it cannot be logically explained.

This kind of meditation is beneficial because it gives us at least a few quiet moments each day. As we increase our intuitive insight, our sense of inner peace increases as well. Stress begins to dissolve, and we face the world and its problems with a new kind of strength.

Daily Life Practice

There is another school of thought that feels that the meditative procedure should not be confined to fifteen or twenty minutes a day. Rather, a different type of what can be called meditation may be carried on through our daily activities. Whether at work or play, we can incorporate our search for stress-reducing inner tranquility into all our daily activities. As before, we do everything the same; the difference lies in our perception and approach to doing it. This is called daily life practice (DLP).

I have found that this approach has great appeal for pragmatic Westerners; consequently, it is more effective. We like to do things, to be active, and to see results. And DLP allows us to incorporate a kind of meditation into ordinary, daily routines.

Two aspects of DLP are especially pertinent to us, as they

give us the opportunity to apply them frequently. The first we will discuss now; the second is discussed in the next section.

The third patriarch of Zen, almost one and a half millennia ago, said it clearly and distinctly: "The Great Way is not difficult; it only avoids picking and choosing." That message still holds true today. We can enhance our intuitive abilities if we avoid picking and choosing as much as possible.

Why is this so? We are aware that our intuitive nature is already within us; we don't have to go outside ourselves to seek it. We also know that the reason it is difficult to "be at one" with our own nature is that something is in the way, and that "something" is our sense of "self," or "I," or our conscious ego. One of the functions of our ego consciousness is to "pick and choose." "I like this, but I don't like that. I must have one, but cannot tolerate the other." If we can diminish this attitude, we can lower the barrier imposed by the "I," and allow more of our inner intuitive nature to emerge.

This is not to say that we should totally eliminate choices. As human beings, there are certain conditions necessary for our existence. We need proper temperature, clothing, food, shelter, and other basics for normal life. Furthermore, this doesn't mean that we should avoid decision making. If I don't like blue, I'm not going to buy a blue suit. Nor should I live in a room whose decor makes me feel uncomfortable.

However, as we go through the day, we are often confronted by situations where things don't quite go our way. "I had a taste for steak, but the group I was with decided on a seafood restaurant." "She was supposed to meet me in the morning, but changed it to the afternoon!" "I asked for Escoffier sauce, but all they had was A-1!"

There is a beautiful Eastern expression known as gracious acceptance. There are times when it just happens, often by chance, and frequently through no one's fault, that we don't get what we want, or must accept what we don't want. Rather than feeling cheated, complaining, becoming glum, sulking, or expressing our feeling in a distasteful manner, gracious acceptance is better for our companions, as well as ourselves.

This is, in fact, another form of something discussed in traditional Buddhism—reducing our unnecessary attachments. Disliking one thing and favoring another are forms of attachment. If, in our daily lives, we can begin to perceive that some picking and choosing is really not important and to accept things graciously, life becomes more pleasant for those around us and for ourselves. Nitpicking, fussy, overly demanding behavior reveals a personality that is dominated by a tyrannical ego that is afraid to allow any of the outside world in. An accepting, open mind that distinguishes between important decision-making and trivial attitudes marks one whose inner intuitive nature is in control.

And now, for our usual question: Does it work? Can we really, by trying to minimize unnecessary picking and choosing in our daily lives, allow our intuitive spontaneous selves to emerge? As before, we defer to the Buddha's answer: "Try it, and see if it works." There is much to be gained if it does, and nothing lost if it does not. Once again, our American pragmatism coincides with this wisdom of the East.

Zen and Performance

There is another aspect of Zen that contains potential promise for those who choose to pursue it. It introduces a unique link between the philosophy/religion and our daily endeavors.

A few years ago, I belonged to a bowling league. As I have previously noted, I am not athletically talented, so my average score was near the bottom of the list. However, I enjoyed the companionship of those in the group, and looked forward to the weekly matches.

One evening, however, something unusual occurred. On this particular day I was late leaving work and did not have time to eat dinner or relax prior to the game. As a result, I arrived at the bowling alley mentally and physically exhausted. When my turn came, I released the ball without thinking. It was a strike! A series of strikes followed, and the alleys grew quiet, with most of the other players watching as I seemed to be heading for a perfect game. I missed one throw, making a spare instead, but finished with an almost perfect score.

In the next game, I concentrated intently, controlling each

step and trying to duplicate my success of a few minutes earlier. To quote the *Miami Herald* sports page the following day: "His almost-perfect game was followed by a humbling score of 99 on the next."

What had happened? Why, when so exhausted mentally and physically that I could not think, did I do so well? And why, when I concentrated on each move and release of the ball, did I revert back to my usual poor performance? If "I," that is, my conscious self, was not throwing the ball, who was? Was it my subconscious, or unconscious, or were my mind and body working on automatic?

While driving a car, have you ever suddenly realized that you don't remember driving the past few miles? Most people have. Furthermore, this automatic driving has been good driving. Whether on the highway or in city traffic, skilled operation of the automobile has taken place. So again, we may ask the same question: Who was doing the driving?

The best answer lies in the book *Zen in the Art of Archery*, by Eugen Herrigel. He was a German philosopher who went to Japan to acquire an understanding of Zen by learning archery. At the same time, his wife studied flower arranging, seeking the same goal. The book describes his training with a Zen master of archery. His perseverance and determination were rewarded; he mastered archery, and reached satori.

The heart of the matter is this: No matter what the activ-

ity—be it music, art, sports, a profession or trade—there is a
state of achievement wherein it becomes so perfected through
practice and a certain mental attitude, that it seems to function independently of the performer. In addition, what is being done is very well done, and apparently without effort.

For pianist Vladimir Horowitz, playing Beethoven seems
effortless. By contrast, most other pianists are straining and
working hard. An outfielder leaps into the air to make an "impossible" catch. A skilled mechanic can listen to the sound of
the engine and surmise what's wrong. A housewife/mother
who deftly cares for her child while at the same time keeps the
household running smoothly, seemingly without effort, is in
this group. We recognize what is happening, and admire it. It
doesn't have to be called Zen, which is, after all, just a name.
Most people who have achieved this level of ability have
never heard of Zen.

Zen and the Martial Arts

The martial arts, swordsmanship and archery in particular, offer an excellent illustration of the application of Zen attitudes
to our daily lives and activities.

Samurai warriors were noted historically for their excel-
lence in combat. It was said that a swordsman could cut his

opponent's head off so swiftly and cleanly that the victim was unaware of what had happened until he moved and his head fell off! An undoubted exaggeration, but it makes its point.

How is this skill developed and perfected? It requires relentless repetition and practice of the techniques, great patience, a skilled tutor, and total concentration on each move. There are no shortcuts. Long hours of daily practice, extending into months and years are needed. Discouragement and feelings of failure must be faced and overcome.

But this does not fully answer the question. All trainees of the martial arts practice their skills continually. What makes the Zen-trained samurai superior? The answer is subtle but profound: the working of the heart.

We normally see our opponent and ourselves as two different entities, and try to outthink and outmaneuver him, to anticipate his every move so that we may counter it effectively. But suppose that a samurai has come to the stage in his Zen aspect of combat that he senses himself at one with his adversary? The split second that it takes to guess what the other is going to do is now eliminated, and it is that split-second advantage, where there is no hesitation at all, that makes the difference. This is what decides the outcome.

The swordsmanship master cannot teach this to the student. He may teach him technique and skill, but not the sense of oneness. This must come to the pupil on his own, just as the stories we related in the Zen monasteries have shown. The following story further serves to illustrate the concept of teaching by not teaching, or the transmitting of a skill.

Matajuro, the young son of a famous swordsman, was disowned because his father believed him incapable of continuing the tradition. He went to one of the greatest swordsmen, Banzo, and asked to become his disciple. At first he was refused, but eventually the master consented to train him. For the first three years the student learned nothing whatsoever about swordsmanship. Instead, he functioned as a servant; he carried water, made the fire, prepared and served the food, and cared for the garden. He became despondent because he felt himself no closer to his life's desire.

One day, however, as he was bending over the fireplace, Banzo crept up behind him, and hit him with a stick. Thereafter, night and day, Banzo's stick unexpectedly appeared to attack him. From this Matajuro acquired a sense of instant response to avoid or counterattack. Eventually he became the greatest swordsman in Japan.

Far Eastern art frequently uses a scene to illustrate our relationship to this sense of oneness. The ocean is shown as a series of peaking waves; Japanese drawings in particular favor this theme.

Let us imagine the sea with a series of pointed waves about to crest on the surface. A given wave may "see" itself as a separate entity; the other waves are "others," and all are totally unaware of their common whole, the ocean beneath. So for a moment, each wave exists, in its own perception, as something separate from the others. This is a false perception on the part of the wave, and Buddhists feel that when we think of ourselves as unique individuals only, then we, too, are misled by illusion.

"All things come into being, they exist for a while, and then cease to exist." This is a keynote maxim of Buddhism. Whether we think of a distant galaxy, a human being, or a rose, the same truth applies.

We all see ourselves as individuals, with our own lives, possessions, and desires. If one can begin to sense a certain unity joining us, such as the ocean beneath the separate waves, then the mind is opening to what is already there. Lewis Thomas, the well-known doctor–author, sees all life on Earth as a web or membrane with all forms related to one another as various manifestations of life force. Similarly, if we are able to diminish our ego conscienceness, a similar awareness will grow in us.

What can we do to free ourselves from our own egos so that we can improve our performance in whatever we do? We know that the first step is to perfect our abilities to the utmost, and hone our skill to the finest edge possible. This takes work, and practice.

The next step, subtle but crucial, is a change in the approach to the work at hand. Let us begin with a simple task such as sweeping the floor. Customarily, our approach will be:

"I am going to sweep the floor." The emphasis is on the "I." Suppose we put the emphasis on the work to be done: "The floor needs sweeping, and I'll do it." Is there a difference? Yes, the difference is that the accent is on the work that needs doing, and the "I" who will do it is secondary. The job is the same—I'll pick up the broom and do the sweeping either way—but the perspective from which it is seen makes the difference. This may seem a minute, unimportant difference in approach, but it is not. Whether the task is a floor that needs sweeping, or an engine that needs to be repaired, or a symphony that needs to be played, or a baby that must be cared for, the change in emphasis from the "I" to the work that needs doing makes a difference.

A good friend of mine is a dentist. He knows little, if anything, about Zen, but I enjoy talking to him about his profession because he illustrates what we have been discussing.

Although he has practiced for many years, he frequently attends postgraduate seminars and enjoys sharpening his skills. What impresses me even more is something he has told me more than once: "When I first began to practice, I felt that "I" was doing the work. I filled Mrs. Smith's tooth, or I treated Mr. Jones' gums. But, as the years pass, I begin to feel that it is the work that needs doing that is important, and that somehow, it is being done through me." My friend is not given to philosophical or spiritual learnings; in fact, his nature is one of scientific and mechanical interest. And as his patient, I can bear out what he says. He is quick to recognize the problem at hand, and to know what needs to be done. Then he proceeds with such sureness and smoothness that his capability cannot be denied. He practices a sort of "Zen" dentistry.

This brings us to those qualities by which we may recognize one who has reached this level of performance. The samurai of the past and some present day achievers share much in common.

The Magnificent Seven is a movie based on the Japanese classic, *The Seven Samurai.* A group of gunfighters is hired to defend a small Mexican village against repeated raids by bandits. The conduct and behavior of the seven, in particular the leader, remarkably demonstrate the qualities shown by a samurai. But what is more important to us, these same characteristics are demonstrated by those few who have reached the highest levels of achievement in their field, whatever it may be.

Perhaps the first facet of character to be noticed is modesty. A true samurai is reluctant to fight, even when provoked to the extreme. A loud bully may challenge him to combat, but even then he resists. He has no need to prove himself to others. Only if pushed to a life-threatening situation will he respond and then, with very few movements, the fight is over.

Similarly, anyone who has acquired this level of proficiency has no need to show it off. The writers, attorneys, doctors, professors, and all those I have known whose expertise in any field has risen to the highest level, are almost uniformly unassuming and modest. They have mastered their field, and don't have to advertise that fact. Their quiet authority speaks for itself.

The second quality to be observed in such a person is the consistent search for improvement. One cannot reach such a level, and then rest. As with satori, the first instant of awakening, it is only the beginning. Mechanic or musician, homemaker or honor student, the skill is maintained not only by practice, but by a continuous search for new challenges. Mentally or physically, as new horizons appear, they are eagerly approached.

A sense of effortlessness in performance reveals the mastery of one who has become one with his or her work. It is here that the sense of spontaneity has emerged. The flow of Itzhak Perlman's violin music is in this sense not much different from Chris Evert's tennis game. The years of practice have flowered to a stage where it all just occurs, seemingly without effort. The violin bow or the tennis racket moving just as it should, without every stroke having to be thought out, is the culmination of tiring and exhaustive practice. Here again, the "I," or the conscious ego, does not appear to be in charge. The playing, whether the concerto or the tennis game, is being done, and done well.

"Less is more" is one of the pillars of Zen. Along with, and related to effortlessness, is the quality of simplicity. A brush stroke on the artist's silk screen, the thrust of the samurai's sword, or a haiku (a poem of only seventeen syllables) reveal the Zen concept of minimizing. As our modern lives grow more complex, as our choices and options multiply, it is here, more than ever, that the Zen quality of developing our intuition becomes increasingly valuable. As confusing issues cloud our judgment and make correct decisions more difficult, the ability to cut through extraneous information and get to the heart of the matter exceeds any other consideration. The more complicated anything is, the greater the likelihood of error.

Humor, in the sense of a self-confident good nature, is often the hallmark of one who has mastered his work. Perhaps it is because the ego consciousness has been somewhat reduced, and whatever has taken over now bears part of the burden. The tensions and strain are diminished, and there is a definite ease in the performance. Few problems can throw him, and the work just gets done. I have seen this in the carpenter who does repairs in my house, and in my dentist. The work flows; there is a harmony in it; the doer is at one with what he or she does.

Remarkably, this entire concept of Zen and performance has a reciprocal aspect that is unique. If one masters an art, one also masters himself; by mastering oneself, one masters the art. To put it another way, by becoming one with the art, one achieves satori.

If we approach our work with a Zen type of attitude, then both the quality of the work improves, and our understanding of our own true nature can mature. It is this understanding that brings us the stress-reducing inner quiet and tranquility that enable us to face the hectic world.

Sooner or later, we ask ourselves whether everything we see and do is material and superficial, or is there within us a sense of the eternal which resonates in our activities? To the extent that we learn to override our ego, we can allow this sense of the eternal to emerge. Taking a Zen approach to our daily activities is one practical way to do it.

Soto Zen

In a small village in Eastern Europe lived a man of considerable wealth. Although he gave generously to the poor, and supported charities as befitted his financial status, he was shunned and disliked by everyone. The reason for this was his own dislike of people, whom he treated with disdain. He avoided conversations, and was curt and abrupt with everyone. Eventually, he felt himself so ignored by the other villagers that it began to bother him, and he turned to the community rabbi for advice.

"I give generously to support those who need it," he said, "but I am disliked and avoided by everyone. The truth is, I do not like people, and it is difficult for me to be pleasant. What shall I do?"

The rabbi replied, "Even if you feel that way about people, act as if you did like them. Smile, greet them courteously, and wish them a warm farewell. Your inner feelings may be different, but treat everyone as though they were truly your friends."

The wealthy man followed this advice. At first he was acting, his pleasant exterior did not reveal his true feelings. But as time went on, his inner self reflected and eventually became what he was portraying. Furthermore, the villagers responded so warmly to his new behavior that it reinforced his changed personality, and he became a beloved member of the community.

How does this story relate to Zen? It reflects the position of the school of Zen known as Soto.

There are two main schools of Zen active at this time. Both are descended from twelfth and thirteenth century masters, at a time when influence was shifting from Chinese Ch'an to Japanese Zen. To this point we have discussed the Rinzai school, which relies heavily on the koan, mondo, strict self-discipline, and sudden satori, or insight.

Soto teachings in Japan have a greater following than Rinzai, but are less familiar to Westerners. The end is exactly the same—insight into one's own nature—but the approach, while similar, is considered gentler, or as sometimes described, more feminine.

Rather than placing all the emphasis on the goal of sudden enlightenment, Soto masters teach that if one is trying, through meditative efforts, to achieve a serene mind, then this action itself is part of the enlightenment. Since the inner nature is already within us, the striving to realize it and the actual illumination are one. Whether it comes as a gradual or sudden insight is secondary in importance to the fact that we are doing something to achieve it.

This concept is illustrated in the story of the wealthy man. Since he was already behaving as though he loved humankind, he was already becoming what he was seeking. Similarly, if we are trying to find this understanding, we are, in a sense, at one with our goal. The effort, the process, and the goal itself blend into a single entity. Zen seems to have a saying for every occasion, and this one, one of my favorites, is particularly apt to this situation: "All life is a journey, so why hurry when you're already there?"

This variation of the Zen approach to self-understanding offers us another option to consider. Stress, tension, and anxiety confront all of us on a daily basis. There is no doubt that self-awareness can defuse these destructive forces and minimize their damage. But we are all different, and some methods work better than others. Those who are ardent goal-seekers may feel disappointed along the way if no progress is apparent. Soto shows that there may be a developing inner illumination occurring simply by going through the process. The doing itself is of value.

If we prefer to allow time for daily meditation, if we get into the habit of avoiding picking and choosing, if we follow a daily life practice, if we relate our search to our work, sports, or other activities, or use any other methods described, something does happen. Whether the recognition of our true inner nature comes gradually or suddenly is secondary to the fact that we are trying, and the effort itself is part of the goal.

Zen and the Arts

Although Zen represents a small percentage of the Buddhist population of Japan, its influence is overwhelming. Both historically and in modern times, almost every facet of the culture reflects this philosophy–religion.

Zen art may be a springboard to further understanding.

As we might suspect, there are certain values that reveal themselves in every Zen artistic expression. Simplicity, the less is more concept, is primary. Secondly, the sense of spontaneity is frequently revealed. At the same time, a laborious devotion to a skill or art to the point where it seems to perform independently is evident. Self-discipline and ritual are important. These qualities are learned along with the art, and show themselves not only in the work itself, but in the developed character of the artist. We recall that while Herrigel was learning Zen by studying archery, his wife was doing the same learning ikebana (flower arrangement).

A Japanese man had a close friend who was a renowned artist. He asked him, as a personal favor, to paint a picture of bamboo, which is a favorite object in Far Eastern art. The artist agreed.

Six months passed, and the man had not yet received the requested painting. Finally, the man reminded the artist of his promise. At that, the artist assembled his ink, brush, and paper. Quickly the brush danced over the parchment; within a few minutes a splendid painting of bamboo with accompanying calligraphy appeared. After thanking him, the man asked the artist why he had to wait six months for something that took but a few minutes to create.

At this, the artist took his friend into his workshop, and showed him a wall covered with more than a hundred similar drawings. The meaning then was clear. Just as the swordsman or archer practices until the skill becomes effortless, the artist had followed the same Zen principle. Through tireless effort, he had reached the point where it was done spontaneously. *The art goes straight from the heart to the brush and paper, without passing through the brain.* There is no thinking involved. Most good Zen art is done in a very few minutes. Minimum brush strokes evoke all there is to be portrayed in a technique called "thrifty brush" and "frugality of ink." Less is indeed more, and the empty part of the paper is as important as the painted part.

Ikebana, or flower arranging, is another art form which reflects the Zen love for simplicity and quiet elegance. The tea ceremony (cha-no-yu), developed by a samurai warrior in the sixteenth century, is a highly ritualized ceremony, and to this day plays an important part in Japanese society. It also emphasizes purity, simplicity, and a serene atmosphere to allow for deep appreciation of beauty and inner tranquility.

The Noh drama, the renowned Zen Gardens, and numerous other aspects of Japanese culture reflect a Zen heritage. Haiku, a poem which contains only seventeen syllables, is notable for expressing the most by saying the least. Basho, regarded as the outstanding Haiku poet, wandered through Japan in the sixteenth century, writing as he went. After a difficult winter in the cold north, he returned home and wrote:

My hut in the spring
True, there is nothing in it
There is everything!

Zen in Everyday Life

A psychiatrist friend has told me that the most important question he can ask a patient is, "How do you feel about yourself?" How we feel about ourselves governs most of our interpersonal relationships and affects our outlook on life.

If a person feels bad about himself, that is, worthless, useless or just no good, then the world appears threatening and hostile. If something good does happen, the person feels nondeserving, and will sometimes unconsciously negate the praise or reward, thus reinforcing his negative self image.

Frequently, such a person will turn inward, afraid to expose himself to any potentially unfriendly situation. Others build up defense mechanisms, such as cultivating an abrasive or offensive manner that is designed to repel contact with others. Such responses will adversely affect any potential or existing relationship.

At a recent philosophical seminar, the subject matter involved feelings and emotions, as well as certain Freudian concepts. A physician in the group stated, "I have cut into many brains in my practice. I have never seen an emotion, much less an id or an ego."

His view of the human being is mechanical, materialistic, and behavioristic, as though humans were puppets, and if the right strings are pulled, one will behave in a certain way. If you can't see it, it isn't there. Over the years I have come to believe that such a viewpoint is like a seven-year-old denying that there is such a thing as adult human sexual love. Since it is impossible for the child to experience it, for the child it simply cannot exist.

When we seek to increase our intuitive perception through Zen, sooner or later we come to see that there is more to human life than our five senses can convey. Although we have only our everyday life to work with, we begin to transcend that which our senses tell us and feel that there may be more. At this moment, we become what in Buddhist literature is called "one who has gone beyond."

Let us now return to the person who feels bad about himself or herself. This sense of isolation and separation from the rest of the world because of a self-image of unworthiness generates undesirable behavior. But from the very moment we experience a sense of being a part of the universe, something changes. We are no longer alone, and we begin to alter our feelings about ourselves and therefore our behavior.

This is not to say that Zen is a substitute for psychological or psychiatric therapy. It definitely is not. What does happen, however, is that the me-against-the-world image starts to fade. The tension and anxiety caused by that image diminish as well, and stress becomes more manageable and easier to deflect or absorb.

A Zen master noticed that one of his disciples had done nothing for several days but sit in the meditative position. When asked the reason for this, the student replied, "I wish to become a Buddha" (acquire Buddha nature). At this, the master sat down beside him, picked up a brick, and began polishing it with a stone. After a while, the student asked what he was doing. "I am polishing this brick into a mirror," was the reply. "But no amount of polishing will make the brick into a mirror," exclaimed the student. "And no amount of sitting with your legs crossed will make you into a Buddha!"

And no amount of sitting will bring about the changes we desire. We must *do* something if we wish to pursue the goals we have described, goals that affect our work, our recreation, our relationships with others and, most of all, our deepest understanding of our own nature, from which springs the tranquility that we all require.

It is said that before one becomes interested in Zen, the mountains are mountains and the rivers are rivers. During the study (or process) of Zen, mountains are no longer mountains, and rivers no longer rivers. But once one has achieved satori, or begins to become enlightened, mountains are once again mountains, and rivers once again become rivers.

This picturesque statement is true. For most of us, everyday things are just everyday things. When we begin to exert effort to alter our viewpoint, things do seem changed from their usual appearances. But when, through sudden or gradual insight, a breakthrough occurs, the everyday things are once again everyday things.

But not quite! Things appear the same, but our awareness of them is forever altered. Those who have gone through this are generally reluctant to speak about it, since it is truly incommunicable, and even the most articulate generally find words useless when attempting to describe this experience.

Our Town

The play by Thornton Wilder contains the best expression of the fruits of Zen that I know. And yet it is probable that Wilder never heard of Zen. Certainly none of the characters in the play ever heard of it, since it takes place in the small town of Grover's Corners, New Hampshire, in the year 1901. This is true Americana, and the Far East is light years away.

The play was first performed in 1938, and the story and the stage are simplicity themselves. There is no curtain, and no scenery. The play opens with the stage empty, and the light dim. The stage manager (narrator) places a few chairs and two tables on the right and left sides, and the story begins.

Human values are revealed in their most basic form. Emily and George are two children who grow up in neighboring houses, go through school and a courtship period, and marry.

Emily dies in childbirth. Act three, the last act, takes place in the town cemetery. The dead are talking amongst themselves when Emily arrives and joins them. She asks to return to the town for one day, and is warned against it. Nevertheless, she chooses her twelfth birthday.

In her kitchen, she sees herself as a girl, but is unseen herself. Her parents are young again, doing the usual daily activities. She calls on them to be really aware of each other, saying, "Mama, just for a moment we're happy. Let's look at one another." Emily realizes then that we go through life without really looking at one another or, in fact, really being aware of the small everyday pleasures. "Clocks ticking, food and coffee, sunflowers, newly-ironed dress, sleeping and waking up. . . . O earth, you're too wonderful for anybody to realize you."

> Then addressing the stage manager, she asks: Do any human beings ever realize life while they live it?—every, every minute?
> Stage manager: No. (He pauses.) The saints and poets maybe they do some.

Zen is only a word. But if it can help us realize life while we live it, it deserves our understanding.

6

Peace of Mind

If looking within one's own heart, one finds no cause for self-reproach, why should he worry, what shall he fear?
— C O N F U C I U S

T HE STUDY OF Confucian teachings is of value to us because it enables us to gain understanding into the Far Eastern mind. We not only benefit by adapting the fruits of their wisdom to our personal use, but we also gain by obtaining a perspective of their general behavior and outlook.

When a Chinese businessman smiles and says yes, but really means no, is he being dishonest? If a Japanese diplomat agrees to consider a proposal, and a year later nothing seems to have been accomplished, is his behavior less than honorable? In each instance, the answer is no.

In both the political and business arenas, we Westerners have certain criteria for our behavior. Bred into us through centuries, we assume this to be the accepted norm throughout the world. Our naivete and a certain amount of arrogance has cost us greatly. We are not only unaware of the differences between Eastern and Western behavior, but until recently there was very little attempt to learn about and to understand them. Our diplomatic and corporate envoys are inadequately prepared, and frequently but unknowingly offend their Asian counterparts. The fruits of this behavior take their toll more and more, as the world becomes smaller and our dealings with the Far East increase.

The Confucian philosophy—religion illustrates one of the major differences between Eastern and Western mentality. We think in straight lines. A is A, and B is B, and never the twain shall meet. We have our own religion, our particular philosophy of life, and our individual opinions. These may change or evolve, but to hold two diametrically opposed views simultaneously is just about impossible in the West.

As shown earlier, quite the opposite is true in the East. The Chinese and Japanese, among others, hold true to two, three, or even four religions simultaneously, with no sense of conflict. And, as we will see, the religions are not only dissimilar, but often 180 degrees apart in concept.

We are already familiar with Taoism, which began in China about 500 B.C. The central theme, a go with the flow approach to life, spontaneity, being at one with one's own nature and with heaven and earth, sets the tone.

If we were given the task to devise a philosophy that totally opposes the nature of the Tao, it would be very much like Confucianism! And yet the Chinese have been Taoists and Confucianists for almost twenty-five hundred years, as well as Buddhists for at least two thousand years.

Language plays an important part in this ability to accept different views harmoniously. Western languages, such as English, with its twenty-six-letter alphabet, lend themselves very well to scientific precision and accuracy. It is remarkable that the same words can range from poetry to analytical description with ease; our thinking relates to our language, and we prefer a succinct approach in most situations.

Chinese letters number in the tens of thousands, and the language is ideographic, based on pictorial symbols. This leads to a communication form that is more vague and symbolic than ours. Problems in translation arise, as scholars are apt to find different meanings in the same words. But there is a richness and subtlety here that the Chinese value and admire. It is frequently this indirect approach to matters that we impatient Westerners find annoying, since we prefer to be concise and to the point. But even one example of an ideograph will illustrate the beauty of the imagery. The ethical concept of morality is pictured as a symbol related to that of the heart.

Having become a little more familiar with a basic difference between the civilizations of the two hemispheres, we may now take a closer look at Confucianism. The politics, government, art, and philosophy of China, Korea, and, to some extent, Vietnam, had been Confucian until their Communist takeovers. Japan is a highly Confucianist country to this day, and if we wish to understand its people, we must have some knowledge of this philosophy.

Confucius

K'ung-fu-tzu (Confucius) lived in the state of Lu, in China, from 551–479 B.C. This coincides approximately with Laotzu, founder of Taoism, who was also Chinese, and the Buddha, born in India. All three major religion–philosophies began about 500 B.C.

Grand Master K'ung, which is the translation of his name, was a magistrate and a teacher. His function was to travel to various courts, instructing the rulers in proper moral conduct and behavior. A following of loyal disciples grew over the years, and when he finally settled down, his teachings continued to the extent that at his death, his students had become a nucleus capable of disseminating his ideas of government, politics, the arts, and personal ethics. These teachings dominated the culture and politics of China until recently. Other countries, Japan in particular, are also highly Confucian, and it is impossible to understand their behavior and attitudes without having some knowledge of this philosophy. Chairman Mao of the People's Republic of China vilified Confucius, claiming his teachings perpetuated an unjust society that favored a small ruling class and masses of hungry peasants. However, Confucius' direct descendants, the seventy-sixth generation, live to this day in his home village of Qufu, which has been spared so far by the People's Republic. Upon his death, some of his disciples mourned for two years at his grave. He was truly the most important Chinese in history.

The concepts of Taoism, traditional Buddhism, and Zen are so far removed from our Western approach to life that we really needed to make room in our minds to accept them. Not so with Confucianism. It is a practical belief, based on common sense and decency. If our previous studies have dealt with our inner selves, we now consider our outer aspects. We meet people daily and interact with them. In a family, business, or social setting, interpersonal relationships must be faced. At the same time that we are seeking inner serenity, we must address the outside world.

Confucius set up a practical, working lifestyle that reflected and was in harmony with our inner selves. There are no holy places, churches, or clergy in this belief. This usually prompts the reasonable question, "Why, then, is it called a religion?" The answer is that it contains two elements directly related to religions: ancestor worship, and a belief in heaven.

The root of Confucianism, in fact, what Confucius called the root of all moral virtue, is *filial piety*. This is defined as the sense of gratitude, honor, and respect due to parents by their children. In a household, the smallest unit of social structures, it is proper for children to act accordingly to fulfill these obligations. The courtesy, manners, and duties to be followed are laid out in minute detail in Confucius' writings.

But it is not a one-way street. The parents are equally obligated to perform their functions of child raising, such as seeing that their offspring are properly fed, clothed, educated and instructed, and protected. Again, these duties are described in detail. Relationships between various family members (for example, between the oldest son and his younger siblings) also require that specific duties be carried out.

This explains why the crime rates in China, Korea, and Japan are extremely low. Anyone disgraced by performing a crime shames not only himself, but his immediate and extended family, and his ancestors as well.

Filial piety also accounts for the unusually high scholastic achievement rate of Asians raised in the Confucian tradition. Whether or not they are inherently more intelligent is debatable, but their hard work at school and long hours of study reflect well upon the entire family. Again, not to do one's best would be to disgrace them. This respect—and respect is the key word here—is also shown to teachers, who are honored as parent figures. In Japan, whenever a student meets a teacher whether inside or outside of school, he or she bows. These Confucian values exist very strongly to this day, and they profoundly influence the behavior of the Oriental whether in his own country or abroad.

Having established a system of moral behavior within the family, the same concepts are now elevated to the local community, the town or village. Filial piety still sets the tone. Now the community leader becomes the parent figure, due the respect, honor, and obedience one shows to one's parents. But he also has an obligation to perform his moral duties well, to administer justice, and protect the members of the community according to the proper code of ethics as laid down in the Confucian writings.

And finally, the same ideals are raised once more through the larger states, and to the emperor himself. In the political sense, the emperor is the parent, and all the subjects are the children. Filial piety is still the primary virtue. There is mutual obligation once more; the subjects must reflect their respect and honor for the emperor according to their status, but the emperor must govern justly and wisely. He must earn their obedience by protecting them in times of war and famine, by seeing that his magistrates administer justice fairly, and by fulfilling his duties according to the Confucian teachings.

It is here that two noteworthy concepts of Confucianism become evident. If the emperor does not live up to these obliga-tions, then it is the right of the populace to rebel, and replace him with a more righteous ruler. This has happened more than once in Chinese history.

The concept of heaven plays a major role in this context. Whereas in our Western world heaven is a place where peo-ple who have led a good life on Earth are rewarded in the af-terlife, the Far Eastern concept is much different. In any social contract, from the smallest family unit, through the vil-lage, in the larger state, and to the empire itself, the following view is held: If the parent or parent figure governs wisely, and the children or subjects live according to the duties and oblig-ations designated, then peace and harmony will result, within the family unit, or the state, or the empire. This good fortune, on any level, is a sign that heaven is with them.

On the other hand, if the parent or child, or emperor or populace do not conform to the basic tenets of filial piety, then discord, unhappiness and, on a larger scale, war or famine will result, which indicates that heaven has withdrawn from them. Heaven is either near us or remote from us, depending on the behavior of those involved. Whether a parent or em-peror is cruel or foolish, or a child or subject is unruly or dis-obedient, a change must be made for heaven to bring its harmony and peace once again to the unit of social structure. Confucianism is considered a means to create a unity between heaven and man.

Why Arno Stopped

Early every morning, I take a walk with my dog, Arno. He is a large German shepherd, with a rather serious expression. This is due to a dark vertical line between his eyes; it gives him the look of one with a concerned frown. If I am to deliver a seminar or lecture on that day, I rehearse it while walking, sometimes talking out loud. Arno is, therefore, a knowledgeable dog as well, since over the years he has learned about Tao, the Buddha, Zen, etc., as well as about some of our Western philosophies.

Recently, on a clear, cool morning, I was silently preparing a full-day seminar to be delivered at the University of Miami. The subject was Confucianism, and I had come to the point now being discussed. Suddenly, I burst out laughing. Arno stopped in his tracks and looked back at me. I shall always recall his expression, and I am sure he was thinking, "All by himself, and he laughs out loud! The old boy must be losing it!"

What was so funny? I was about to discuss the questions that a Confucianist must find answers to if he wishes to follow the path of morality. I had vocalized inwardly:

How do we know who we are?

How do we know where we come from?

How do we know how we should behave?

How do we know what heaven (God) expects from us?
I can give you the answer in one word . . .

It is here that I began to laugh, as I realized that I had prac-
tically quoted the opening dialogue from the well-known mu-
sical, *Fiddler on the Roof.* Tevye, the poor milkman in a small
Russian village at the turn of the century, is asking the same
questions. He turns to the audience and says, "I can give you
the answer in one word." Those who are familiar with the
theme can hear the crescendo of the background music as
Tevye shouts, "Tradition!"

It is indeed tradition that powers Confucianism. The history and classics of the ancient sages are considered to represent a sort of Golden Age that should be emulated. Knowledge
of this wisdom was considered essential to govern, so all offi-
cial positions were to be filled by those who could pass a test
about classic values and traditions. These tests were given
once a year, and applicants arrived from all over the empire
in hopes of qualifying. Those who passed could become government officials in their home districts. This system of civil
service examinations continued until 1911, when the last dy-
nasty, the Ching, ended and China became a republic.

Knowledge of Confucianism requires understanding three
basic concepts. The first is a word much favored by Confucius
himself; he spoke of it frequently. The word is "jen," and it is
the source or wellspring from which filial piety springs. If fil-

ial piety is the root of moral virtue, then jen is the root of filial piety. Jen simply means human-heartedness. That an entire philosophy–religion rests on such a simple concept as
love, goodness, and human-heartedness makes it endearing to
me. A natural flow from the human heart is the source of other
human virtues, such as loyalty, as well.

Li is the second concept we must understand. It has to do
with propriety, or behavior. The rules of conduct, which number 3,000, and the rules of ceremony, of which there are 300,
provide the basis that enables one to carry out precise actions
in response to specific situations at any given time. Confucianism is a practical philosophy in the sense that it answers
the question, "What do I do now?" When confronted with a
particular situation, the details of how to behave are already
proscribed.

Yi, the last of the three basic concepts, has to do with the
duty or obligation to carry out the embodiment of what is fit-
ting. It is simply doing what must be done. In Christianity, it
is sometimes equated with Christian charity, a basic mandate
of behavior. In Judaism, we find this quality in the righteous
man; he cannot behave in any other way and still identify
himself as a member of his faith.

The basic tenets of Confucianism described here provide
another key with which we may unlock the mysteries of Far
Eastern culture. Its influence on history up to and including
the present is immense. The customs, manners, and behavior

of the Japanese, Koreans, and Chinese are derived from the Confucian background. Things are done in a certain way simply because that is the way they are done.

A "Working" Confucianism

And so we once again return to the core of this book. Are there values in Confucianism which have a useful application in our daily, pressure-driven and tension-filled lives? And once again, the answer is yes.

What can the wisdom of Confucius deliver to us now, in the closing years of the twentieth century? To answer, we may quote the Master himself: "Peace of mind." What better bulwark to erect against the ravages of stress than peace of mind? This gift ranks with the inner harmony of the Tao, with the enlightenment of traditional Buddhism, and with the intuitive grasp of one's own nature of Zen.

Confucius refers to "that most precious possession, peace of mind. If looking within his own heart, one finds no cause for self-reproach, why should he worry, what shall he fear?"

Ralph Waldo Emerson's essay "On Compensation" is a work that rests alongside my copy of Omar Khayyam's *Rubaiyat*. It is worth rereading periodically because it helps us confront what appears to be a paradox. Emerson refers to a type of situation where we compare two men. One of them works hard, assumes responsibility, is basically honest, cares for others, and has respect for basic moral virtues. The other is a schemer who is dishonest and who will cheat when it will benefit him, and who does not care for the feelings and well-being of others.

The paradox appears when we see the man with moral values struggling through most of his life, while the schemer seems to have the biggest car, flashiest girl, and much more of the material rewards of the world. It seems unfair. The conclusion that both Confucius and Emerson present is that the peace of mind that results from the moral behavior of the first man is the balancing factor.

This may be a difficult concept to swallow, given the moral climate of recent decades. *Winning Is Everything, Looking Out for Number One* . . . these books and others like them reflect nothing new. It is simply the old philosophical question, "Does the end justify the means?" No matter whom you must trample to get there, let the sweet smell of success lead you on!

I paraphrase an oft-quoted saying written, I think, by a well-known sportswriter a few decades ago: "When you arrive at the big playing field up yonder, they won't ask whether you won or lost, but how you played the game." The end does *not* justify the means; it is how you achieved your goal that determines your real worth.

Moses Maimonides (The Rambam), a twelfth-century philosopher, reflected upon this enigma. He believed that when the world treats one unfairly, or if life sometimes seems unjust, the problem arises from the fact that no human is able to comprehend the full scope of what is happening. An Indian story tells of a man who had two possessions, a son and a pony. One day the pony strayed away, and the man was unhappy. A few days later, the pony returned, bringing with him a beautiful white stallion. The man was overjoyed, especially when his son mounted the stallion. However, the son fell off the horse, and his leg was broken. The father was once again distressed. In a few days, however, the king's army officers came to the village to recruit forcibly all the young men in preparation for a war. Because of his broken leg, they did not take the son. Of course, the father was now very happy again.

The point of this story is, of course, that we cannot make judgments based on single incidents or individual situations. Maimonides said that only God knows the entire scope of events, and what appears to be unfortunate now, may turn out later on to be for the better. A Taoist might reason in a similar vein; the Tao cannot be understood or described, so we cannot know how things will be. A Buddhist might claim that the man was too attached to the events. His seesaw of happiness and unhappiness depended on what was going on; true happiness comes from within.

This is not meant to be a Pollyanna approach, that somehow good can be found in all things. Nor do we wish to sound like a morality play. Innocents do suffer, illness strikes good people, and wickedness may go unpunished. What Confucianism does proclaim is that if we, personally, adopt a sense of morality, kindness, and certain social graces such as respect, then we will be at peace with our inner selves, and will have no cause to feel shame or guilt.

Westernized Confucianism

The practical application of this philosophy on a day-to-day basis may be looked upon as an exterior reflection of the peace, security, and harmony we are developing inwardly. Both within and without, our mental processes and social behavior begin to evolve into a formidable antistress barrier.

Lord Kenneth Clark, in his remarkable television series, "Civilization," concludes with a personal view on courtesy, one of the foundations of Confucianism. "It is a ritual by which we avoid hurting other people's feelings by satisfying our own egos." As with all truths, it is quite simple. Furthermore, it is a good point of reference. If we pause momentarily, before an act or statement, to reflect on how this will affect the other person, we can avoid hurting both them and ourselves.

In addition, courtesy is the child of respect, and respect is really what it's all about. In Japan, China, and other Confucian countries, respect for one's parents is the top priority throughout life. Filial piety in action is wonderful to behold;

it is the cement that holds the family and the community to-gether. This respect, this expected behavior, extends to all family members.

And it extends to the elderly in the family and in the com-munity. It has been shown that longevity and health in the later years of one's life are directly related to the community's accepted perception of age. If, as in many Western countries, older people are made to feel useless to society and are ex-pected to wither away in retirement villages or nursing homes, the stress upon them biochemically and physiologically takes its drastic toll through illness, chronic depression, and sui-cide.

But if a community respects its elders, as Confucianism teaches, and they are made to feel useful, part of the family, and a source of wisdom and experience, their lives are longer, happier, and they usually die peacefully in their sleep. Watching the grandchildren while parents work, being con-sulted about family problems, and being treated with honor simply because they have experienced life's difficulties, are some of the best remedies for stress in the elderly.

Respect—for teachers and educators, and for knowledge itself—is the reason for the high percentage of Far Easterners in the ranks of highest scholastic achievements in this coun-try. We all know struggling parents who run a Chinese restau-rant or laundry, and we know that their children, if of age, are in college. When a Japanese or Chinese student meets his teacher outside the school, he bows in respect. Sadly, we have areas in our country where, in a similar situation, the teacher considers himself or herself lucky if they are not assaulted. There are two Confucian attitudes at work here. One is respect for the teacher, and for the parents and family; the other is that to do anything less than their best is to dishonor all those involved.

There are other aspects of respect as well. Mutual regard exists between the employer and the employee; each acknowledges the position and value of the other. The chief executive of a Japanese factory has his steel desk right on the floor so that the workers have easy access to him; he is not in an unapproachable, top-floor suite.

And, of course, the overall interpersonal manner of behavior is based on courtesy. No one wishes to behave in a way that may cause the other to lose their dignity or face. This is why a Chinese or Japanese will seldom answer with an outright no. They will express disagreement a little later in a more respectful way that lets you know how they feel without hurting your ego.

None of us can be expected to immediately adopt these behavior patterns; our Western and, in particular American, ways are much more abrupt, direct, and to the point. This comes naturally to us, and it is part of our way of getting things done. But we can certainly modify our behavior to show more courtesy and respect. If at the same time we are acquiring a more tranquil inner self, there will be less need to be brusque, impolite, or inconsiderate. Whoever our interpersonal relationship is with—a family member or loved one, or a friend, or a supervisor or a coworker or a subordinate—thinking about what we do or say to avoid hurting anyone is beneficial to them and to ourselves.

The purpose of adapting some of these Confucian values to our own day-to-day style of living is the same purpose as that for which the philosophy was developed: A strong family unit gives us a sense of belonging. Respect for others, especially those who need it and deserve it most, gives us, to quote the master, "priceless peace of mind." And most of all, behavior of this kind is an outward manifestation of that which we are seeking—an inner peace that diminishes and absorbs harmlessly the daily onslaught of stress to which we are all exposed.

In this era of the rat race, trendiness, and a sort of constant semihysteria, words like dignity and poise may seem out of place. But the fact is, these qualities are more important than ever. "If," as Kipling said, "you can keep your head when all about you are losing theirs and blaming it on you," you are a rarity, and a valuable one at that!

It is said that the ideal in the Taoist tradition is a saintly hermit, and in the Confucian, a good citizen. Can a person in these times possess an inner peaceful harmony, a courteous, self-confident manner, and still have the drive and ambition often required to succeed in life's daily pursuits? Absolutely! Overtly aggressive behavior, rudeness, and insensitivity to others' feelings are not requirements for success; they are, in fact, deterrents. The Japanese are a prime example; their immense success in the business and financial world is constructed within a framework of civility, courtesy, and respect—a reflection of their highly Confucian society.

7

Getting It All Together

A contented person is never disappointed. Those who know when to stop do not find themselves in trouble. They will stay forever safe.
— T A O - T E - C H I N G ,   V E R S E   4 4

E VEN WHEN I don't have an appointment, my dentist friend invites me to his office from time to time to show me some new equipment or technique. His enthusiasm is contagious. I can't help sharing his pleasure in a technological breakthrough or knowledge acquired at a postgraduate seminar. He truly personifies the concept that a professional man must be a perpetual student.

On my most recent visit, however, he concluded by saying something that had meaning beyond his intention. "Arthur, with my new technology and research information, I can now solve almost any problem my patients may present!"

To repeat what was presented in the introduction, one way to look at life is to see it as a series of problems. To solve these problems, we need as much information and as many techniques as we can acquire. The purpose of this book is to enhance our ability to confront these problems and, by doing so, to reduce the damaging effects of stress upon our lives. We have gleaned from the Far East the essence of their wisdom, and are now better prepared than before.

The Buddha's last words can become the basis of our efforts: "Strive with diligence," which means we have to keep working at it, "and be a lamp unto yourselves," no one is going to do it for you. We alone have the power to free ourselves from stressful onslaughts. But it takes some perseverance and determination to do so. Are the results worth it? Our pragmatic experience answers a firm yes!

What exactly are we seeking? Let us revisit that highlight of the Buddha's life once again. In the classic scene, he is seated beneath the Bo tree, about to achieve enlightenment. Mara, the mythological god of the underworld, has sent up armies, spirits, and his seductive daughters to frighten and distract him. These attempts fail, and there is nothing that can prevent the Buddha from acquiring his insight, and realizing the Four Noble Truths.

Why? Why were Mara's threats and temptations destined to

fail? Because there was no one there! Although physically the Buddha was sitting in the cross-legged meditation position beneath the tree, mentally he had arrived at a state of complete nonattachment, or nirvana. He saw himself not as an individual, but as a part of the entire universe. (In Zen terminology, he had gone from small mind [the individual] to great mind [the entire universe or the Tao].)

What had changed was his self-image, how he perceived himself in relation to the world. It is extremely unlikely that any of us will arrive at such a point of total detachment, but it is very likely that many of us will reach some degree of insight. Herein lies the value of Far Eastern thought: If we substitute stressful situations for Mara's attempts, then we can deflect or absorb the stress by the same change in perception. We are simply not there.

Here we arrive at a paradox: How can we be here and not be here?

Much of the humor in Zen derives from the concept that life itself is a paradox. A story is told of a young monk who smugly told his master that he had achieved illumination and was now aware that he was nothing but an illusion. Recognizing the foolishness and arrogance of the student, the master gave him a hard blow to the side of his face, saying, "If you are nothing but an illusion, then why is your cheek turning red and why are you so angry?"

Can we late twentieth century Westerners live with such a

paradox? We are not in an isolated monastery; we are in a highly technical, materialistic, active society where most of us must get up, dress and eat, and prepare to face daily challenges and frequently stressful situations. The paradox is not as difficult as it seems to be, once we begin to see ourselves as part of the universe, rather than outside of or opposed to it. Once we alter our self-perception, things begin to flow differently.

It is possible to maintain the active, even sometimes aggressive and driving kind of energy necessary to make it in today's world, and at the same time possess an inner serenity and tranquility that immunizes us from much of the tensions and anxieties.

Our New Perceptions: A Review

Having acquired an initial grasp of the four philosophy–religions that shape the Far Eastern mentality, we should review them in order to clarify and reinforce their beneficial adaptation to our daily lives.

The Tao
Life on Earth goes back three and one-half billion years, and everything within us derives from this hereditary chain. Every cell and organ in our body is preprogrammed to perform spe-

cific acts and functions. Modern medical research is just now beginning to understand this amazing phenomena.

And certain rhythms are built into us that reflect not only ourselves, but all life as well. Our social structure and civilized manners, more often than not, do not coincide with these natural rhythms. Were we meant to eat three times a day at certain intervals? If we suddenly feel tired at three in the afternoon, is our body telling us it's time to rest while the clock in the office says there are still a few hours of work that remains to be done? Obviously, our body's activity pattern is often out of sync with the working world's demands.

When asked for advice, a master replied, "When I am tired, I sleep; when hungry, I eat." This may work in a monastery, but it won't work in most of our lives. What we need is a compromise.

It is for this reason that the value of the Tao to us Westerners increases at the same rate that our lives become more complex, for the Tao keeps us in touch with our own true nature while we pursue our day-to-day routine.

The te, our own personal portion of the Tao, is really our own inner nature. As we discussed earlier, our lives are happier and smoother when we follow that inner nature. It is nothing less than the wisdom of our bodies speaking to us.

P'u, the uncarved block, is the Tao's message of simplicity. The more complex our lives appear to be, the more we should think of Thoreau's "simplify, simplify." To cut through problems and reduce them to their basic factors is the surest road to solving them. Winston Churchill refused to read long, complicated reports. "The only thing they assure," he said, "is that they will never be read." Excess gadgetry complicates our exterior lives; too much inner complexity alienates our basic natures.

And wu wei, the concept of doing by not doing, becomes more valuable by the day. The more we are swept up by busyness, by filling every moment with work, recreational activity, or a driving desire to achieve something, the more we should remember that doing nothing is often the best option. Sigmund Freud, who in his lifetime contributed voluminous knowledge to the world, treasured his times of total relaxation. He said that much of his work was done while he was "doing nothing."

Buddhism

Learning to view life with the perception of a Taoist gives us a more placid and tranquil inner self. Learning to use the Buddhist attitudes enhances and reinforces our ability to cope with external stress.

First, know that what needs to be done, we must do ourselves. Second, learn to modify, when necessary, our perception of the world.

Nonattachment is the outstanding quality to be sought in

applying Buddhism to our modern daily lives. To restate it in another way, we should avoid unnecessary attachments. Once we identify what is truly important in our lives, we may begin the process of weeding out the rest. Our loved ones, our work, our home, and a few other attachments are necessary in most of our lives. But many things in our lives are not really important or worth worrying about. We should reconsider the ideas and things to which we are attached and abandon those which are unnecessary.

What is the reward for this? Recently I found myself at a business affair, exposed to an increasingly noisy, rude, argumentative, and generally distasteful group of people. I felt my wa, that is to say my inner serenity, being disturbed; in Western terms, my stress level was ascending rapidly. I mentally focused on an image discussed earlier—a lotus, cool and unattached, floating on the dirtiest of waters. This Buddhist concept (as we recall, the Buddha is frequently portrayed as sitting upon a lotus) enabled me to diffuse the stress. Physically, I was still there, carrying on with the common amenities. But emotionally I was like the lotus flower, disengaged.

The value of this self-training is immeasurable. And, as the Buddha said in one of his most pragmatic messages: "Try it, and see if it works. There is nothing to lose, and much to gain."

Zen

Furthest removed from our Western mentality, Zen seems difficult to grasp since it is arrived at by intuition rather than by logic. It requires an inner discipline and self motivation far beyond that of most other pursuits. But, as discussed in Soto Zen, the attempt itself is part of the goal. In one sense, the path and the goal are one. Avoiding picking and choosing puts us in a frame of mind which brings us closer to understanding.

The application of Zen principles to our work is of immense value. To perfect our skills to the point where they seem to perform by themselves and to grasp intuitively what to do next, are the signs of a master at his or her craft.

To return again to the concept of life as a series of problems, we find that the ability to cut through complexities instinctively is a skill well worth developing.

Some readers may enjoy confronting the koans and mondos; others may meditate in the traditional or daily-life methods. Whichever method we choose, there is much to be gained and nothing to lose.

Confucianism

The exterior behavior reflecting an inner tranquility is revealed in the courtesy, consideration, and respect inherent in the Confucian tradition. The image of the lotus flower floating on the pond helps us to be calm in the midst of discord and confusion. The Confucian ideal, persons of moral character and responsibility, lives in our culture today. Ladies and gentlemen still exist; we know them by their manners and behavior.

"For East Is East, and West Is West"

"And never the twain shall meet" wrote Rudyard Kipling. Was he right? For the most part, yes. It will be centuries before the general population on either side will begin to understand the other and to exchange attitudes and beliefs. The Japanese enjoy Coca-Cola® and baseball, and we like sushi and Japanese electronics, but these are superficialities.

Inroads are made daily, however. As the world shrinks, our economic and political ties draw us ever closer, and understanding is sure to increase.

But on the deepest religious, cultural, and philosophical levels, progress is much slower. This book is an attempt to bridge that gap, specifically because there is much to be gained from Eastern philosophies by us Westerners, particularly as our lives become more filled with anxieties, tensions, and stress.

In the West, treatments for anxiety and stress fall into two general categories, self-help groups and books, and traditional counseling.

Popular psychology is fundamentally superficial, and deals with quick-fix solutions. "Recipes" is the term sometimes applied to this sort of treatment. For a given set of circumstances involving interpersonal conflict or distress within oneself, a formula is offered to solve the problem. At times this can be effective with varying degrees of success, and it may be useful in short-term crises.

Traditional therapy is the field of the psychiatrist, psychoanalyst, and some exceptionally talented and trained psychologists. It involves exploring problems at a deeper level in order to uncover the underlying causes of distress and unhappiness. Here the treatment is longer and more costly, but when it is successful, it brings to the patient an understanding of oneself that helps him to weather the storms of conflict both within and without. The results are longer lasting; once certain hurdles are crossed, they seldom return. This is the result of an insight into one's nature, which is one of the goals of Western treatment methods.

But what of the Far Eastern approaches to such problems? Do they work as either pop psychology or as traditional therapy? Actually, the wisdom of the Far East works on both levels.

When confronted with a stress-generating situation, we have a variety of quick fixes that we can use. For example, we may call upon the Taoist concept of flow, and let the unpleasantness go through us as though we were water. Buddhism provides the image of a lotus flower floating pure and serene above the morass; this image then helps us to picture ourselves as similarly rising above unpleasant situations.

Or we may think of the Zen paradox that we are here, but we are really not here; in this case, it is better not to be here. And from Grand Master Kung, Confucius, we have learned to maintain our self-disciplined, calm exterior.

Freud and his successors explore the unconscious, the id, the ego, and the superego. They establish the longer but more certain road to overcoming fear and anxiety by guiding us to an understanding of ourselves.

Self-awareness, knowing who we *really* are, provides the release of tension and stress. Rather than "analysis," a term seldom used in the Far East, we acquire an *intuitive* grasp of our true nature. Knowing this with the same innate wisdom that informs us without formal teaching, we find ourselves with a potent, built-in defense against the "slings and arrows" of daily life. We have a long-term solution to many problems; a resilient "cushion" of Eastern wisdom.

While teaching many classes over the years, I have been greatly impressed by the number of students who have devised their own solutions for visualizing mental images or concepts to quickly alleviate sudden, unexpected stress. Sometimes principles that I had mentioned only briefly, thinking them to be of less importance, had proved effective and beneficial for some students. For example, in an early lecture on the Tao, I said that something as common as a cluster of trees might help one relate to nature. Eight weeks later, during the open discussion at the end of the course, a woman related that she has always liked a particular group of trees near her home; she now imagines herself standing among those trees when she feels threatened or alone, to her immediate benefit.

We all vary greatly in what affects us or has a special appeal to us. Any particular image, saying, or concept that seems to have special meaning can be stored and held for a future useful application. (My favorite is a Zen quotation: "All life is a journey, so why hurry when you are already there." When I find myself being pushed or harassed, it helps me to slow down and to sort things out.)

Although "recipes" are useful in getting us through stressful incidents, the most important and valuable wisdom to be acquired is that which changes our perception of the world and our place within it. This is a consistent, constantly deepening awareness that forms a protection against the onslaught of stress, anxiety, loneliness, and low self-esteem.

When a stress-producing event occurs, what is damaged is our sense of self. If, as the wisdom of the East can teach us, we are able to lessen our sense of "self," there is less of a "target" for stress. Lessening our self does not diminish us, it enhances us. The small "self" actually becomes a part of the great "Self." Earlier we spoke of "small mind" becoming "Great Mind." This is the same happening. Nothing is really changing, except for our image of ourselves. No longer a small, isolated individual who needs constant "pumping up," our ego threatened constantly by external events, we become an integral part of the universe, no longer alone.

"Certainly It Hurts"

Lawrence of Arabia, while a British Army officer in Cairo during World War I, would sometimes hold a burning match between his fingers and allow the flame to touch and burn them. He showed no sign of pain at all.

When questioned by a fellow officer as to whether it hurt, his reply was remarkable. "Certainly it hurts. The trick is not minding that it hurts!" This reply is understandable to one familiar with Zen. Lawrence was saying that it is possible for a person to detach oneself from mental or physical pain. Those who are advanced in Zen and mental self-discipline are able to do this in various degrees.

The search for freedom from stress will be only partially successful. Prolonged illness, physical pain, personal losses, financial crises, and role changes such as retirement, result in anxieties, depression, and varying degrees of physical discomfort. No one can change this.

But if we have acquired some insight into ourselves, we are better prepared to face stressful occurrences as they arise. Furthermore, on a day-to-day basis, we are able to filter out minor stress-producers, such as rudeness, noise, and other such irritations. A psychiatrist friend of mine once compared this state of stress relief to shutting off an air conditioner that had been constantly running. We had become so used to the background noise that we hardly noticed it, but when it ended, it was a quiet, restful relief.

Which Is Better?

The most frequently asked question at the end of my lecture series is this: "Which is better, Western culture or Eastern culture?"

This is a poorly worded question. Neither is better; both have desirable attributes. Certainly we should be proud of our Western heritage. I consider myself a cultural descendant of Socrates and Plato, Newton and Einstein, Beethoven and Mozart, Michelangelo and Van Gogh, Darwin and Freud, and countless others who lead the way in the arts, sciences, and political concepts which enrich our lives.

But we cannot ignore other great cultures which have produced their own arts and philosophies. I feel we should open
our minds to different ways of viewing things. And above all,
as Americans and pragmatists, it should be important to glean
from other cultures that which will be useful and beneficial to
us, without diminishing our Western heritage.

In parting, for those readers who choose to acquire some of
the wisdom of the Far East, I can offer no better advice than
that of a Zen master who taught many centuries ago:

> *When you stand, stand;*
> *When you walk, walk;*
> *But above all, whatever you do,*
> *Don't wobble!*